OREGON FEVER

An Anthology of Northwest Writing

1965–1982

OREGON FEVER

An Anthology of Northwest Writing

1965–1982

Edited by Charles Deemer

Avellino Press
Portland, Oregon

©2005 Avellino Press
All rights reserved

ISBN 0-9643408-9-5

Library of Congress Cataloging-in-Publication pending

Cover photo of Mt. Hood by Joe Gault Bianco
Cover and book design by Mary Margaret Hite

Avellino Press
PO Box 8454
Portland, OR 97207
503.223.6737
jrbmedia@hevanet.com

In Memory of
EDWARD M. MILLER
Managing Editor, *The Oregonian*
1965–1970

CONTENTS

TWO: THE PLACE

PREFACE

The stories in this book were written by prominent and not-so-prominent Northwest writers. They were first published in The Sunday Oregonian's *Northwest* magazine (Portland, Oregon). Permissions to reprint here were obtained from the writers. I revived *Northwest* magazine in the late autumn of 1965. I remained its editor until 1982. The stories were selected by Charles Deemer, a Portland author and playwright, and a frequent contributor to *Northwest* magazine.

The reasons for publishing this book are many. Most important to me is to show the freedom that I enjoyed as a working journalist for *The Oregonian*, one of the most prestigious newspapers in the west and the country.

I loved the magazine and I knew it was loved by the readers. The reader was my critic, the one I looked to as a measure for our success. If I satisfied the reader I was doing what I had been assigned to do. I felt I accomplished that.

However, the personality of the magazine could not have evolved without the unflinching support and encouragement of Edward M. Miller, managing editor of *The Oregonian*. He gave me the opportunity.

I will not forget my loyal staff members who steadied the reins for me. They were the ballast. Ted Mahar, Paul Pintarich, Bob Michelet, Connie Hofferber, Jim Magmer, and others shared with me the high points and the dry spells. I thank them most sincerely.

None of this, however, could have been accomplished without my bosses, and to them I say "Thank you." Most importantly, I will always be indebted to Editor J. Richard (Dick) Nokes, who made my journey at *The Oregonian* one great trip.

So sit back, enjoy some of the young upcoming authors of that period, some of whom eventually reached national acclaim and to this day are writing some of the best literature in America.

Joe Bianco
Portland, Oregon

INTRODUCTION:

NORTHWEST MAGAZINE AND THE OATMEAL MIND

Charles Deemer

On a Friday evening in fall, 1965, Joe Bianco answered the telephone to find Managing Editor Ed Miller on the line. Miller told the Agriculture Editor that he wanted him to revive *Northwest* magazine, a Sunday supplement *The Oregonian* had published some years before, with Miller, Jalmar Johnson and John Armstrong variously working as its editors. Bianco accepted the offer. But on Monday morning Bianco hurried into Miller's office and retracted his acceptance. However, Miller wouldn't take no for answer. Suddenly Joe Bianco was a magazine editor.

On paper, the Agriculture Editor looked like an unlikely choice for such an assignment. Bianco had come to *The Oregonian* somewhat reluctantly in 1955, thinking of Portland as a stepping-stone to San Francisco. Only a few years out of college, he'd already established an award-winning reputation in Harrisburg, Pennsylvania as a crime reporter. He'd been nominated for a Pulitzer Prize for solving a case involving serial murders on the Pennsylvania Turnpike. Without college training in journalism, Bianco, a history major, became known as an aggressive, hardworking investigative reporter. He'd come west to Oregon because his wife was from here and to find new challenges.

Tired of police work at *The Oregonian*, Bianco became Agriculture Editor in the late 1950s. Once again he quickly made his mark, exposing the realities of migrant labor life in a series of articles he wrote after posing as a worker in eastern Oregon. Bianco's work received national recognition:

"It took months of preparation," said an article in *Editor and Publisher* (a newspaper industry magazine) on August 12, 1961, "before Joe Bianco, Agriculture Editor of *The Oregonian*, was able to assume the role of a migrant farm worker for a week. His portrayal resulted in a series of three articles which aroused the interest of state and federal authorities concerning the plight of these people."

Bianco, Miller must have thought, was just the kind of high-energy, fearless investigator who could turn the bland supplement *Farm, Home and Garden* into a general features magazine, something more widely readable.

When Miller refused Bianco's retraction, the new editor asked if he would be free to make all editorial decisions for the magazine. Miller gave him free rein.

What happened in the next few years was the gradual evolution of *Farm, Home and Garden* into *Northwest Home and Garden* into *Northwest* magazine. A number of important benchmarks were reached along the way.

Bianco's first challenge was to bring feature articles into the existing supplement, initially placing them in the back of the magazine behind the home and garden stories. He tried to lure Oregon's best freelance writers to contribute, but in the beginning this was an uphill struggle. Oregon novelist Don Berry, suggested as a contributor by Bianco's artist wife, finally agreed to send him something—and then dared him to print it.

The story that Berry submitted was entitled "Kultur in Apathyville." Earlier *The Oregonian* had run a story about Portland's cultural life and Berry's story was a direct challenge to this appraisal. The problem was more with the audience than with the artists. Portland, he wrote, was the "last and finest bastion of the oatmeal mind," a place where culture was nothing more than somebody talking "arty over cocktails." Oregon artists and writers, many with national reputations, were not appreciated here at home.

Bianco kept the story in a desk drawer for weeks. He expected to be fired if he published it, but his wife encouraged him to publish it anyway. Finally making his decision, Bianco told his editorial assistant to prepare to take over the fledgling magazine. Next week Bianco expected to be looking for a job.

Berry's article created a firestorm. Letters to the editor

poured in—both for and against the opinion. Subscribers cancelled the paper, and even *The Oregonian*'s editorial page criticized Berry and Bianco, one section of the paper reprimanding another. However, Bianco's immediate boss, Ed Miller, supported him and the editor kept his job.

Berry's article encouraged formerly reluctant writers to submit to the new magazine. Portland's Rick Rubin, a writer with credits from *Esquire* and *Playboy*, submitted an article that *Northwest* published only one month after Berry's piece—and which created yet another controversy.

In "Westside, Westside, All Around the Town," Rubin argued that only downtown Portland represented "the essence of Portland." Folks who lived eastside over the river were merely "necessary to our continuing intellectual and cultural growth, much as the slaves of Greece in the Golden Age were necessary to support the more meaningful few."

Most of the paper's editorial writers lived across the river and didn't appreciate Rubin's attitude. In only four issues, as 1965 ended and 1966 began, *Northwest* had created two firestorms of controversy—and the voice of Miller's dream of a resurrected magazine was born in a feisty, sometimes irreverent and always challenging brand of journalism, enthusiastically nurtured by the new editor.

Early on, this style of writing was relegated to the back pages of the magazine. The primary content continued to be about home and garden. Then the focus and appearance of the magazine began to change.

1966 started with a slight name change, to *Northwest Home and Garden*. Interestingly enough, at this time there was no masthead to identify the editor at the helm.

At the end of 1966, Bianco wrote a short editorial introducing a new format and title for the magazine. Finally he was identified as the editor. "Features" became the first section of the magazine, receiving primary billing, with the home and garden stories now following behind. This was the format that would define *Northwest* magazine as it moved into the '70s. In April, 1976, an Arts section was added. Six months later, a poetry page.

By 1969 *Northwest* magazine already had gained national attention. In an article called "Not For Oatmeal Minds" in the May, 1969, issue of *Quill, the Magazine for Journalists*, James J. Doyle wrote:

"Much of *Northwest*'s high-voltage has come, and has been retained, by its dynamic editor Joe Bianco. Trained in the hard school of East Coast dailies, Bianco works from the premise that this country is undergoing a great social upheaval—a potentially rapturous calamity which calls for investigation and social analysis beyond the scope of newspage content. What has resulted is an open forum of ideas for freelance writers and professional reporters."

A 1967 survey identified *Northwest* magazine as the most popular and widely read section of the newspaper. Ed Miller explained to Doyle: "I suspect a large share of our readers pick up the section now with the subconscious query, What the hell is *Northwest* up to now?"

About his handpicked editor, Miller said, "Bianco has a talent for picking today the controversial subjects of tomorrow."

One of the ways *Northwest* brought these subjects to its readers was through frequent theme issues, in which a series of articles would look at different aspects of the same subject matter. The content of theme issues varied widely, including:

- *practical subjects*—a gardening issue each spring, a skiing issue each fall, periodic Northwest travel issues.
- *current events*—hippies and the counter-culture in April, 1967; student revolts in January, 1969; the gasoline crisis in August, 1979; a royal wedding issue in August, 1981. (In 1980 Bianco edited *The Oregonian*'s book about the eruption of Mt. St. Helens, which sold almost 250,000 copies.)
- *social and political issues*—abortion in March, 1969, and again in October, 1979; family violence in February, 1977; Oregon's rural poor in July, 1968; the role of the church in the urban jungle in December, 1980; the changing family in May, 1981; victims of rape in July, 1981.
- *issues not receiving wide attention*—cults and deprogramming, an ambitious three-issue series in July and August, 1977,

largely written by Bianco himself; Portland's air pollution in August, 1973; the gay lifestyle in April, 1975; blacks in the community in January, 1968, followed by a special issue on the black woman in January, 1972; the controversy surrounding Portland's downtown redevelopment in December, 1973, with a magazine proposal for its own priorities of development; and even a behind-the-scenes look at *The Oregonian*'s own power structure in February, 1979.

About the special issue on the hippies, Doyle wrote: "...before the hippie sub-culture had its own periodicals, *Northwest* blasted the minds of editors and readers with a cover story on the burgeoning pop culture, light shows and hippie enigma. At the time, few national magazines had examined this phenomenon to such an extent."

Doyle concluded his *Quill* article by writing, "But *Northwest* has proved beyond all doubt that a magazine can grow and develop and reveal the controversies that readers seem to want more and more, time and again. It has also proved that readers in what was once an easy-going and folksy town, have less fear of social icons than newspapers normally presume."

Don Berry had ended the article that catapulted *Northwest* into public consciousness with advice to those who were happy with Portland's gray complacency: "Don't make waves." *Northwest* magazine—even as it offered advice on home and garden, even as it wrote in praise of the Oregon landscape and offered travel tips over the state's back roads, even as it profiled interesting Oregonians known to all or unknown by many—never ran from controversy or avoided a new challenge. *Northwest* magazine was where the action was.

In the summer of 2004, I spent many hours preparing this book by going through the archives of *Northwest* magazine. Even though I had been a regular contributor myself for a time, much of the history of the magazine was unknown to me. After my first issue-by-issue inspection of the archives, 1965–1982, I found myself with a list of several hundred stories I wanted to reprint. Clearly I needed criteria by which to retain and eliminate stories. I also wanted a device by which to communicate the wide field of interests in the magazine, yet without producing a book too large to attract average readers. I finally decided to organize the stories into sections: People, Place, Issues and Concerns, Sports, History and Nostalgia, Arts, the Lighter Side. My strategy for suggesting the abundance of material in each category was to reprint a few stories in their entirety and provide excerpts from many more.

The most challenging section to put together was Issues and Concerns. Here was the very heart and soul of *Northwest*'s primary thrust, the source of most of its controversies, and yet here, too, was the material most topical and in need of contextual explanation to be appreciated by contemporary readers. Soon enough, however, I identified the issues I should focus on—because these same issues still face us today. The stories here about the Environment, Civil Liberties and the Changing Family, which were published by *Northwest* magazine between 1969 and 1981, could have been written today.

Our title, *Oregon Fever*, comes from the affliction attributed to families who would abandon everything at home in the East or Midwest to take to the Oregon Trail in a sudden search for a new beginning, a new life. A similar journey and mindset informed the journey of *Northwest* magazine and its adventurous writers and readers. This was an exciting era, as anyone who lived in it will tell you. *Northwest* magazine was both a product of and an instigator of the times. What resulted was a magazine that attracted writers like Don Berry, Rick Rubin, Barry Lopez, Thomas Gaddis, David Shetzline, Ivan Doig, Larry Colton, Larry Leonard, Charles Gould, Art Chenoweth, Daniel Yost, Dorothy Velasco, Paul Pintarich, Beth Fagan, Buck Hannon, Don Holm, Jack McCarthy, Ralph Friedman, Penny Avila, Wyn Berry, Jean Henninger, Ferris Weddle, Charles Potter, Evelyn Yates, Virginia Holmgren and others too numerous to mention, writers eager to participate in such an energetic and era-defining regional forum.

When Don Berry threw down the gauntlet—"Don't make waves"—even he must have been surprised to see how the magazine developed into a newspaper Sunday supplement like none before it and few after, a weekly publication full of good, great and challenging writing, a magazine "not for oatmeal minds." We begin, then, with the two controversial stories that started it all.

KULTUR IN APATHYVILLE

Don Berry

Dear gray Portland, last and finest bastion of the oatmeal mind, where the principal entertainment is sitting around in coffin-like solemnity telling each other what a shame it is that 'nothing ever goes on in this town.' It is our own private pleasure, our masochistic solace under leaden skies, a kind of ritual self-immolation to no discernible end. Not for us the flamboyant dramatic gesture. But we mutter quite a lot.

Occasionally, of course, the old cadaver gives a little twitch, a sort of involuntary spasm (there must be a medical term for this specious illusion of life), but it quickly subsides, to everyone's great relief. A bit ago this newspaper examined the state of culture in the state of Oregon. What a disaster. Most of the writers—with a few marked exceptions—went at it with all the enthusiasm of men assigned to search out maggots in bad meat. They appeared to resent being snatched away from their contemplation of automobile accidents and Friday Surprise goodies merely to see if anything was actually happening in this state other than collisions, politics and other such familiar catastrophes. It was no wonder that the picture painted was of a dismal wasteland, broken only occasionally by a sulfurous bubble of fermentation, probably unsanitary in nature.

And if the newspapers do it badly, television and radio don't even bother with the pretense. Their silence is so total you would think culture had become slightly controversial, perhaps upsetting to potential sponsors. The broadcast media, of course, have the inestimable advantage that their own sins are swept magically away when you turn the set off, while print remains.

In this the mass media faithfully reflect the general attitude of its audience.

Total indifference, tinged with faint revulsion and suspicion. (This, incidentally, can be regarded as an outline of the Portland mentality. Color it gray. Dark gray.)

In fact, it is not the local culture that is impoverished, but the local perception of it. There is an almost total lack of connection between the makers in Portland and the appreciators, with their low moans.

It is my contention that this enormous chasm has been deliberately bulldozed out of the oatmeal mentality in order to protect itself from undo stimulation. Portland determinedly insists that nothing goes on; activity is bad, per se. We resolutely peer at the world through dead-colored glasses which are donned at the least suspicion of a breaking ray of light. Our winters give us the photophobic vision of troglodytes—and apparently our minds, such as they are, are equally affected.

Examples come quickly. I have never met Mr. Don Zavin, but in my mind's eye I picture him as being equal parts naiveté and bafflement. Naïve enough to believe all those nice people who tell him they want some theater in Portland, want someplace to go, something to do. And when he comes up with such—stay home. That's where the bafflement part comes in.

For a while there were two poets in this city simultaneously, each of whom is generally regarded by critics as being among the most important of his generation. Jim Dickey was at Reed and William Stafford was, and is, at Lewis and Clark. San Francisco would have done some fancy feather preening at such a happy coincidence. Portland? Not a ripple. A local columnist, who actively prides himself on searching out writing talent, had never even heard of them.

Where, comes the wistful cry, are the grand old days of Portland writers like Holbrook and Haycox? Where, indeed? How come nobody seems to notice that William Sanderson of this newspaper has as good an understanding of Oregon as Holbrook ever had, and writes as well? And I haven't been deafened by bands playing welcome Janet Stevenson, a writer whose Civil

War novel *Weep No More* is a classic, and whose biography of Fanny Kemble is the definitive one. And, if that kind of stuff is too "lit'ry" for the oatmeal mind, did you know that Rick Rubin was back in town? Who he? He's published fifty-odd short stories in national magazines in the past five years, including *Esquire* and *Playboy* and others even a Portlander might recognize. Of course, Mr. Rubin has a lot going against him in Portland. He has, I understand, both a beard and a beautiful wife, which is unseemly of him. Either, alone, is enough to make a good gray citizen uneasy. He must be a beatnik or something.

The list of people doing important work in this town is too long, I can't get it into this space. And I don't mean regional poets and Sunday painters. I'm talking about people of national stature like Lloyd Reynolds and Jacques Avshalomov and Tom Hardy and Manuel Izquierdo and Carl and Hilda Morris and dozens of others who are so busy working they won't even be insulted I didn't mention their names.

The point I'm hacking away at is this: there is plenty going on in this town, plenty of real work. What is missing is the dilettante fringe, which is what passes for culture in most cities. And it is in fact the absence of the dilettantes that our appreciators complain of. Culture to the oatmeal mind means that they want somebody to talk arty over cocktails, and that's all it amounts to. Pure hypocrisy, which is another of the mainsprings of the Portland mentality.

It's a no-connection city, where reporters talk only to other reporters and politicians to other politicians. It's full of little social daisy chains, self-fertilizing and self-contained. Portland is the living refutation of the old biological principle that an organism cannot survive in an environment composed solely of its own waste products. Mentally, we do exactly that. Not only do it, but glory in it, and stubbornly resist any infusion of fresh air into our bleak atmosphere. If a magazine starts—we kill it. If a theater group struggles up out of the mud—we softly muffle it to death under pillows of leaden silence. The plain fact is that we don't want anything around that might stir up the mush.

I end this rash note to my city with a piece of advice on

fitting in, being a true gray Portlander. I modestly call it 'Berry's Law of Survival in a Bowl of Cold Oatmeal.'

Don't make waves.

12.12.65

WESTSIDE, WESTSIDE, ALL AROUND THE TOWN

Rick Rubin

When one speaks of New York, it is in fact Manhattan that one pictures. Los Angeles, beyond a vague image of smog and sprawl, is really the Sunset Strip, and San Francisco, disregarding a few other points of interest, is enclosed by Van Nuys and Market streets.

Where, then, is Portland?

Need one really ask? Granted that the world's largest small town is not yet and perhaps will never be a real city, what there is of cityhood is West of the Willamette.

True Portland, proper Portland, the essence of Portland, stretches in fact only from Willamette Heights south to Dunthorpe, from the river to the crest or perhaps slightly beyond of the West Hills.

In fact, even when defined as the West side of the Willamette, Portland is a rather more limited state of mind. For Raleigh Hills and Beaverton, New Burlingame and Linnton, however geographically not Eastside they may seem, are not thereby strictly speaking Westside. Illogical perhaps, but true none the less.

What then may a Portlander say of the vast, sprawling Eastside? This enormous flatland of homes and manufacturing plants, parks and minor hills, garish shopping centers and tree-lined streets and roaring freeways?

No doubt it is not the worst possible place on earth to live. For one thing it is very near Portland. One could hardly be so insensitive as to argue that there are not many estimable citizens living there, that certain of the manufacturing plants must not perform some useful function, that several of the parks would not be the cool green gem of any Midwestern city. One would have to be a fool to argue that a spool of thread purchased in Montavilla or Sellwood, St. Johns or Kenton, is any less useful than one purchased in Portland.

One is even willing to concede that errors have been made in the location of certain essentially Portland institutions. What could be more Westside than Reed College, and the scattered pads of the Reedies? The Aladdin Theater, our only true art showhouse, is by some comic mischance over there, as is the wholesale produce center with its truly city sights and sounds and smells and even one or two of our artists lives in murky isolation over there.

But as for the thing that Eastsiders themselves hold most dear, their vast chrome and plastic Lloyd's Center, their frighteningly Los Angeles-like Sandy Boulevard, their view from Mt. Tabor, why your true Portlander holds them as not so very significant. No more than might be found in Middletown or Zenith City.

It is such a flat and characterless land over there. And surely it must be heartrending, traveling antlike hither or yon across the wasteland, to come of a sudden upon a western view, to see our small but intense downtown, backed by our mosaic-patterned West Hills, to glimpse sophistication and real life, so near and yet so far away.

Well then, what about the Westside? If it is the essence of Portland, what then essentially is Portland?

It is the joyous chaos of unplanned variety. We are one of the oldest cities on the Pacific Coast, or at least the oldest not destroyed by fire and earthquake, and our remaining old buildings attest it. Not old by European standards perhaps, but here one senses the flavor of age and urbanity, the gray and gritty mixing with the rich and the flavorful.

Skid Road is here, and the all night restaurants and groceries, here one sees small shops that limp marginally into a perilous future side by side with large and prosperous emporiums. Here are found the used bookshops and here are found the local equivalent of haute-couture, here are the hurrying men with attaché cases and the slower men with beards and large dreams. Men on the last leg of the long downward trip and men on the way up, men with mad visions who shout on street corners and philosophers who stalk the streets with angry grimaces or beneficent smiles. The Westside is city, sound and color, failure and success, the Westside is the unplanned cornucopia of win, lose and draw, but always a little larger than life.

And above it all are the green hills, which come down to caress it, Forest Park and Portland Heights, lush Canyon Road, idyllic Willamette Heights and proud Dunthorpe. Those hills above the city that are uniquely Portland, that make it a city where ten minutes travel from downtown finds you among raccoon and deer, and you may walk where few if any have ever walked. But you will have traveled west, not east.

What is city about this village is Westside. From Burnside and First Avenue to Riverview and Westover, from Slabtown to Goose Hollow, from Macadam Avenue to Vista Avenue. It is a place that grew from private dreams, with all the agony and joy that comes that private way, that time and toil and hurt and hunger can make, and you can keep your slide rule designs and your Lloyd's Center, which strikes the Westsider as handy and necessary, but about as authentic as one of those plaster potatoes they use to demonstrate the cubic capacity of a new refrigerator.

Oh, we shop there at times, but we do not love it.

Your Westsider imbibes his prejudices on the subject of East and West with his mother's milk. He grows up in the rich polyglot of race and creed, class and condition, that marks a city. His high school, by which I mean only Lincoln, is no pasty monochrome of one or at most two classes or colors, but rather embraces every shade and size and shape, an education outside of the classroom as well as in, with cashmere sweaters and dirty blue workshirts, delicate daughters of the finest families and hardnosed streetkids, black and white and yellow, Indian and Gypsy and purest Protestant.

Your Westsider grows up on or at least near city streets, not the placidly pseudo-rural curved avenues and lanes of some suburban tract. And all of his youth he feels the green and motherly West Hills enclosing him, tempering city toughness and spirit with nature's equal opposite.

Grown to adulthood, he finds his way. He may move to San Francisco or New York, he may move to the wilds of Montana, but seldom will he move across the river. Eastsiders may become perceptive and cross the Willamette to rise in the world, but your Westsider feels faintly ill at ease just going across the river for a movie or a hamburger. Don't linger too long, his mind's dark subconscious warns, the all-pervasive gray is contagious.

Do you doubt it? Why then did the Symphony Association worry so when they had to temporarily transfer their sounds across the muddy stream? Why advertise that it was permissible to cross over and hear the music if they did not instinctively know that it went against the Portland grain?

The millionaires live west, and by and large the artists. Scholars and hustlers find their way here, merchants and misanthropes, philosophers and conmen. Bohemia, that mark of cityhood, is almost purely Westside, and far more prevalent than your Eastsider would imagine. Cities are where Democracy is found, and Freedom as well. Here is the library, here was and will again be the symphony, here the art galleries and here the bookshops. Stewbums and social lions live here, agitators and analysts.

But seldom a neighborhood booster, those good gray shopkeepers who sing the praises of their useful but unromantic little districts. Here we grow by ourselves and find our own unhindered way to excellence rather than simply gross receipts. We know that for real shopping one must wander down a street where every block promises a surprise, drift past or into the old shops, following our unplanned noses to unimagined riches.

We shop the Farmer's Market, a sort of anarchy compared to your supermarkets, we seek what we need or love by chance or luck, by rubbing variety's humped shoulder. For entertainment we select Broadway or Fourth Avenue, for clothes we pick between gaudy and glamorous, for living we have the prosperous hills or the seedy neighborhoods of Victorian decay.

Across the river one might as well be in Omaha or Fresno. True, the Oregon countryside still stretches away in its wonderful variety, to ice-cream cone mountains and the raw North Pacific, to fishing streams and hunting hills. True too that for a Midwestern town the Eastside has a goodly number of trees, a plentitude of pretty parks, several pleasant neighborhoods. But so has Zenith City, and flat characterlessness too.

Daily the Eastsiders swarm across our bridges, each evening their off-springs come to rap their noisy pipes west of the Willamette. We know them to be necessary to our continuing intellectual and cultural growth, much as the slaves of Greece in the Golden Age were necessary to support the more meaningful few.

One does not speak of divorcing Eastsider from Westsider. One is only a little sad for the limits of their lives, and occasionally angry when they vote to urban renew away our rich variety, to make it like their extruded plastic uniformity, and freeway down our history. We know they mean no harm, only lack the city man's wider vision.

We pity them even, their inferior climate, the gorge winds blowing hot and cold and always dusty about them. Our views are larger here, our streets more real, our lives richer.

Defined by our river and our hills, sniped at by boosters and earthmovers, the Westside struggles onward and upward, humble and generous and filled with the knowledge that excellence must have its opposite, that every true city must be supported by its hinterland Eastside.

1.16.66

one:

The People

"Mark Allen: Producer, Director, Actor"
by Art Chenoweth
" 'I'm tired of people saying Portland is a bad show town
because of the audiences. Business would be much
better and there would be more theater if people would
stop blaming the audience.' "

———————

"The Thurman Street Thoreau"
by Larry Leonard
*"He is a Roman Catholic and favors birth
control, a World War II hawk, a Vietnam dove, a
Medicare liberal, a law and order conservative."*

———————

"The Poet of Juniper Mountain"
by Charles Deemer
*"His hickory shirt was glazed with dirt as he
stepped up to the bar. 'Gimme a shot of your
rotgut whiskey, and the butt of an old cigar.' "*

3

MARK ALLEN: PRODUCER, DIRECTOR, ACTOR

Art Chenoweth

Mark Allen is a man of wrinkled brow and burning stomach who had dedicated himself to the idea that Portland shall have independent live theater, even though, he says, "It's frightening to look around and realize that I'm alone." In independent production Mark is, indeed, alone. In an unlikely-sounding place called the Friendly House, 2617 NW Savier St., he is producing regular plays of high quality.

It's a former church building and Allen has a lease on the auditorium, which he has converted into a theater. Every Friday and Saturday night he hopes that 84 people will show up, give him a full house and help pay the bills for another week.

Allen does not consider himself in the same category with the Portland Civic Theatre, long-time champ of local community drama. The Civic has a board of trustees, a supporting membership, an allied Guild and along with them a type of responsibility which places it, in Allen's view, in a different role.

"A city can have only one Civic Theatre," he said. "There is only one area the theater can expand in and that is in the area of independent production."

To make his independent theater go, financially, is what gives Allen his wrinkled brow. It is what has put him, at times, on an ulcer diet. But he makes it plain he is in it to stay.

"If any young fellow wants to make money this is not the field," he explained. His wife, Nancy, nodded wise assent. "But," and the wrinkled forehead took on more intensity, "I want to do what I want to do. And what I want to do is theater."

Hollywood-born, Allen always was interested in theater as

a hobby. Even through college he was getting radio jobs, roles in old-favorite shows like "Suspense" and "The Whistler."

He coached inexperienced actors for screen tests and taught at Los Angeles City College. While there, he advised one of his students to forget acting—too wooden-faced—and stick to writing. But Jack Webb ignored the advice and went on to make "Dragnet" a byword in television.

Eighteen years ago, at age 25, Allen learned that some outstanding actors—Lee J. Cobb, Hume Cronyn, John Garfield—were forming an Actor's Lab.

"I thought to myself, why don't I drop around and see if I can help those follows? Maybe give them a hand with the teaching." Mark laughs about it today. "It was a year before they would let me on the stage."

In 1957, Allen learned of an opening in radio here with KPOJ and took it. In 1964, he elected to go full-time into theater.

The Mark Allen Players were born seven years ago with "The Drunkard." While in Hollywood, Mark had enjoyed playing in an old-fashioned "mellerdrammer" called "The Blackguard" and had observed the success of the more famous "Drunkard." The Players did "The Drunkard" more than three years, from 1961 to 1964, and still revive it on occasion.

Bob Sinclair was most often the dauntless hero. Two of the more splendidly nefarious villains were John Hillsbury and John Van House. But it was advertising man Dave Alexander, playing the part of the rube, who created the most gripping scene—at the Oregon State Penitentiary.

Alexander, a hopeless mugger, at one point turned to the cons and yelled, "All right men, when I give the signal it's one-two-three and over the wall." Everyone except Alexander froze—then the cons broke into a wave of chuckles. Allen resumed breathing.

"The Drunkard" expanded into two companies and Allen decided to put one on tour. He arranged once-a-month appearances at four locations: Eugene, Salem, Longview-Kelso and Mount Hood.

Mount Hood? An unlikely spot for regular theater. But at Rhododendron Mark became friendly with Bill and Nancy Spencer, who were operators of the Log Lodge.

The Log Lodge is a devil-may-care hangout which draws the young beer-drinking ski crowd in winter. But in summer Rhody had been pretty dead.

The Spencers whipped up community interest to the extent of more than $300 in backing. The Mark Allen players set up outdoors and the first night played to a standing-room crowd.

The Rhododendron Summer Theatre this year will enter its seventh season, opening at Bowman's Mount Hood Golf and Country Club. With an 8-to-12 percent increase in attendance every year and a dedication to light, sophisticated plays, it appears entrenched.

Phase one for Allen was "The Drunkard"; phase two, the Rhododendron Summer Theatre. Phase three had to be a permanent Portland locale. One attempt was an in-the-round effort called the Actor's Ring at NW 23rd Ave., off Burnside.

Allen, eventually, in his continuing search, learned of The Friendly House, a community center owned by First Presbyterian Church, which had a suitable auditorium. Last November, after six months of negotiations, the Actors Repertory Theatre opened to a schedule of one new play about every five weeks.

One of the most recent, "Death Of A Salesman," with Mark Allen in the leading role of Willy Loman, has been the biggest grosser. Allen first did the Arthur Miller classic three-and-a-half years ago, considers Miller one of the all-time greats and "Death" one of the two great plays of our time. (The other: Edward Albee's "Who's Afraid Of Virginia Woolf?")

Allen's approach to his project draws some of its inspiration from Angus Bowmer, who built an unlikely idea into the highly successful Ashland Shakespearean Festival. A year ago Bowmer gave Allen the germ of his philosophy:

"Formulate a plan and a method of activating it, then devote your life to it."

Let it not be said that Allen is floundering for a plan.

"Arthur Miller said good theater should make common

sense to common sense people," Mark explained. He classifies theater into three areas.

First, the classic theater—like Shakespeare—the kind of thing many colleges are doing. Second, the modernist movement, avant-garde, currently represented by the Theatre of the Absurd.

The third type, what Allen calls the naturalistic theater, is his area. Miller, Lillian Hellman, Clifford Odets.

"I feel my cup of tea is not the theater that depends on the audience going home and spending many hours asking 'what happened?' Not the 'happening' type where you take a nude girl, plaster her with spaghetti, then eat off the spaghetti while colored lights are flashing.

"I like theater that gets you where you live."

One problem with the naturalistic theater is that few serious plays of any merit are being written today, in Allen's view. It's simple economics. With Broadway costs what they are today, producers look for the safe formula—a comedy with a small cast, one set and as much double-entendre in the lines as possible.

Nothing wrong with comedy, Allen emphasizes. But the demise of the serious play depresses him. And it leaves him with a small list to choose from, if he's to follow his "naturalistic" bent.

Portland should be able to support at least three theaters like his, Allen said. As it is, about one theater a year comes and goes. It is on this subject that the furrowed brow becomes colored, heated with emotion.

"I'm tired of people saying Portland is a bad show town because of the audiences. Business would be much better and there would be more theater if people would stop blaming the audience.

"You can't have an audience without first having the doers, and I'd like to see a lot more doers."

College theaters and the Civic Theater have an advantage that brings out a little envy in Allen. It's the spirit of everybody going out and supporting these theaters because they're community efforts.

"Nobody talks about whether we should support John Doe's theater," Allen mused. "Although, maybe it's not a disadvantage. It forces us to quality."

Allen's views are so well-developed on all phases of theater that he probably should one day write his own book.

As for acting itself, he said, "The actor does or doesn't create this thing we call empathy with an audience."

He continued, "Too many people who are potential actors don't want to study the craft. They just want to get up on the stage for the catharsis of acting.

"Acting is a craft. There are tools of tragedy because it can be boiled down, the trade to be developed. Actors don't just happen. The natural actor is fine only for type-casting."

Comedy is much easier to play than tragedy because "it can be boiled down to a science." You play a piece of business and the audience laughs or doesn't laugh and you learn thereby.

Tragedy, the portrayal of tragedy, must be experienced. But how can an actor, particularly a young one, play convincingly emotions of hatred, love, fear?

"There is no person who has not had all the emotional experiences necessary to play any part, although sometimes it is necessary to indulge in magnification."

As an example of magnification, Allen cited the emotion of hate strong enough to kill. Anyone can easily imagine a mosquito biting his arm and experience enough hate to swat that mosquito.

From there you magnify. The mosquito is a spider which will bite you, painfully. Then it becomes a snake, ugly and venomous, about to strike. Kill it! Kill it! And so on, up on the scale of magnification.

"If you can swat a mosquito, that's enough hate, that's enough disregard for life, to play the killer of a human being."

Allen himself portrays grief and shock by remembering the sight of his pet dog, killed when Mark was a child. To the child Mark, that was a tragedy.

"Tragedy is not what a man is about to do or what he has done but his inability to walk away from it and say the hell with

9

it," he said, quoting Arthur Miller.

"It's a terrible thing if someone you know well is killed in an auto. But if you were behind the wheel, that's tragedy."

By this process of recreating, a specific personal tragedy can, for the actor, become any tragedy.

In "Death of a Salesman," Allen, as Willy Loman, is told he has lost his job. How does Allen, as Willy, experience the necessary shock?

"Howard (in the play) says, "You're fired," and I see my dog."

Today Allen looks ahead five years, when he hopes to be debt-free and paying his actors. He wants continual expansion. He hopes for a time when all community theater bands together, with a joint box office, an exchange of posters, a schedule devised to avoid conflicts of opening nights.

He'd like to see an actor's training center. And a sort of hardcore repertory company of six to ten actors. "Then you can develop what is called an ensemble play. It's like dancing. The first time you dance, you're stepping on each other's toes."

All these would be facets of the Mark Allen Theater effort.

There is one thing that Mark Allen does not want. He doesn't want another review like the one he got five years ago after he opened the Kaufman and Hart comedy, "Once In A Lifetime."

The critic, the late Bob Walters of *The Oregonian*, offered these words, which have burned themselves into Mark Allen's soul:

"Mark Allen produced 'Once In A Lifetime' and it seemed that long."

4.16.67

THE THURMAN STREET THOREAU

Larry Leonard

George Cetenich is a lot like the late Will Rogers. He's home-spun, direct, incisive and full of good common sense, a philosopher, if you will. It is risky to dub a man of 73 thus, since men of this age tend to cracker-barrel opinions anyway, but George carries his mantle like a Thoreau: with a grand simplicity.

To meet this philosopher-in-cobbler's-clothing, I went to his shop at the corner of 22nd and Thurman in Portland's industrial district. There, I found a yellowish building of early vintage and uncertain ancestry, wherein labored Mr. Cetenich.

Anyone younger than 25 will have a bit of difficulty picturing the scene that met me as I walked through the door—the oiled wood and the dusty cabinets, the washed amber walls and the odor of tannic acid. When you enter these old shops, it is the combination of sights, sounds and smells that generally go unnoticed that take you back to the post.

The old man turned from his whirring machine and smiled. When he turned, he did not straighten his back, but remained bent: his spine arched permanently from so many decades at the polishing wheel. He will not stand straight again.

Thrusting his thick-fingered hand forward, he introduced himself with an accent that shifted from Russian to Italian but was neither. He is Yugoslavian, from what was then the countries of Austria and Hungary. His face is a broad face, frosted with white stubble and eager to break into a grin or focus a baleful eye while a point is being made.

I asked him what he had seen, where he had been. How was it in the old days, old man?

He moved to the slat-backed rocking chair that commands a fine view of the dusty windows and the people passing by, he sat and speared me with that eye.

"My father," he began, "He say dere going to be a war with Germany, and I should come to the America where it is safe." Which he did, at the age of 17 (the year was 1913). He came to San Francisco to work as a dishwasher for twenty-five dollars a month, seven days and 12 hours per.

He had a trade then but, because he could not speak the language, could not ply it. At the age of eight his parents had apprenticed him to a shoe-maker…so he would not, like the other boys, wander about the town after school causing trouble. He applied himself and learned quickly.

"In San Francisco, when work was slow and I had a nickel, I would go to the big saloons on the waterfront. Hey! The food was free when you bought nickel stein of beer. Ah, spaghetti, salami, cheese— all free! I say to myself, 'Dis is God's country.' "

After several years of railroad work and time biding while he learned the language and customs of his adopted country, and a summer on the north Pacific after salmon, he managed to save $1500, come to Portland and begin his business.

1921 to 1968. That's 47 years in the same place doing the same thing. To last that long in that manner you have to be either incredibly dull or incredibly interested in the workings of a small part of the world. Mr. Cetenich is an interested man.

"My wife, she want me give this up, retire, hey? But age is against me—you been doin' somet'ing all your life—better you stay there than go home and die."

A man walks in; he says he is 82 and he looks 62. By the way he talks, he is an arch conservative and the damned Democrats are ruining this country.

George allows as how that's possible if you include the Republicans and everybody else in that statement. He ponders fanaticism: "That Kennedy—poking around in those sand pile like he was gonna help Israel, maybe. Look what happened. Is nationalism too strong, the world is sometime crazy from it."

Were women different in the old days, George?

"Even in those days you couldn't tell them much."

He sits and rocks in the chair. The sun in smoky November columns rolls languidly across the floor. The thick hands make a popping sound when he slaps his thigh and exclaims: "Hey! That's right. What you think?"

Cetenich on wives: "Women, they getting too much rights—too independent. You say one word, one little t'ing and they split up. End up on welfare. Is bad for the little children."

Cetenich on age: "When you get old, naturally you get a little crabby—a little more crabby, what you t'ink? Maybe woman hurt by t'ings, maybe man too. You got to be more careful."

On hair: "My boy, he spend two years in Tunisia with the Peace Corps. He come back with hair down to here. 'Hey Donny,' I say to him, 'I don't like long hair?' He say that Jesus wore it like that, so I tell him, 'Fine I give you twenty dollar and a new suit. You go get hair cut.' " He laughs a bright laugh and pops his thigh again.

George, are you a citizen of the U.S.?

"Oh, God yes." His short arms lift. He talks with them and with his hands and nodding head like the Italians.

Politics?

"America is becoming socialistic." In his mind, neither good nor bad except in relationship to the situation. He favors socialism in Yugoslavia, is against it on principle here. "The countries in Europe should merge and become like United States. There should be one language, like Esperanto (an international language, artificially constructed from words common to the major European languages). There would be more friendship with more understanding."

Friendship, love and honesty make up the bag in which Mr. Cetenich carries his philosophy. You cannot judge him weak for it, though, because at times you ask him questions and his answers are guarded.

He is a Roman Catholic and favors birth control, a World War II hawk, a Vietnam dove, a Medicare liberal, a law and order conservative. He thinks a man should spend some of what he makes and save some of what he makes. And in these moderations, he parallels the thoughts of a gentleman born some 324 years before Christ.

"There is a road to happiness," wrote Aristotle, "a guide to excellence which may save many detours and delays: it is the middle way, the golden mean."

This fine old Yugoslav has figured that out.

"Hey! What you t'ink?" he says, rising from his chair and pacing through the amber dust to his cluttered bench. "I like to talk more today, but it is late and these shoes must be finished. If they were mens, well we could talk. But womens—hah! That is somet'ing else entirely, hey?"

11.17.68

THE POET OF JUNIPER MOUNTAIN

Charles Deemer

"Can I buy you kids a beer?"

By no means an unusual offer in the Unity Tavern, but this was Memorial Day, 1973, and in a few weeks we were leaving Oregon for what now seems like forever.

Nor, at first glance, did our benefactor appear out of the ordinary. He was a working man, clearly: By the dented hard hat, the sun-toughened leather of his arms and face, the lived-in work clothes.

But later, after the casual conversation that usually follows the gestures of buying and accepting a beer, we were asked a question that took us, for all our English Department degrees, by surprise: "Do you kids like poetry?"

He recited by heart, in a voice that was not ignorant of the dramatic use of pause and rhythm. We didn't know as yet that he was reciting his own work.

"There's an empty seat on the crummy, where used to sit Hooker Jack. In a little bungalow in the suburbs, there's a new widow dressed in black.

"It happened last Thursday afternoon; there was nothing anyone could do. The puncher ran into a hang-up and jerked the mainline in two.

"Jack was up on the landing, tying down a yarder sled, when the spar pole broke at the cheek bolts and crushed a hooker dead.

"So old Jack is in logger's heaven, and many stories have been told, about the cold brooks that trickle by the wayside, and the streets are paved with gold.

"There will be no blocks to carry, and no more haywire to

pull, for it doesn't snow in the winter, and the coffee jug is always full.

"Alarm clocks haven't been heard of and woolen underwear is a thing of the past. So after thirty years on the mountain, old Jack made it home at last.

"We know when at last we join him, he'll have the layout made, and with his coffee jug beside him he'll be sitting in the shade.

"Then old Jack will arise, this logger big and strong: 'I been through a whole jug of coffee; what took you guys so long?'

"Then we'll all gather at the spar pole and sit on the yarder sled, while Jack tells of the new job that at first we looked to with dread.

" 'Up here they only fly one choker and there's four men on the crew. You don't have to wear your hard hats, and your cork boots are shiny and new.

" 'You'd never see a man run to get his self out of the bight, and it's an unheard-of thing up here for a logger to have a hang-up to fight.

" 'The crummies are all air-conditioned; the side rods never come around. The yarders all have mufflers and never make a sound.

" 'There's no such thing as Monday and you'll all get paid every day. The cookshack door is always open to feed each and every stray.

" 'Sometimes I think it's almost too easy for a high-ball logging man, who gave all those years of his life in pursuit of the silver strands.' "

Fred Ross calls himself the Poet of Juniper Mountain. Although he has published in *Loggers World* and in a few newspapers, he is an oral poet foremost, whose stage is likely to be whatever tavern he is in, whose audience is whoever will listen. Let us call him a folk poet then, whose poems focus on the work he knows best:

"I followed the logging game for 25 years. I've logged from the redwoods to the Northern Lights."

Fred describes himself as a tramp logger, as opposed to the

homeguard boys who work steady jobs with families near at home. But tramps aren't bums: "They'll work but they're like boomers on the railroad: They're never satisfied." A good deal of this restlessness is reflected in Fred's logging poems: "His hickory shirt was glazed with dirt as he stepped up to the bar. 'Gimme a shot of your rotgut whiskey, and the butt of an old cigar.

" 'I'm in from the cold where the vine maples grow and the dogwoods bloom in the spring. I've been in the woods for twenty years and I haven't accomplished a thing.' "

Now in his fifties, Fred came to writing slowly. Although he has taken a few writing correspondence courses and has tried his hand at a couple of novels, his discovery of poetry came later, on a day when he found himself on a crew with much younger men.

"I told the foreman, 'Man, I can't keep up with that buncha racehorses,' " he said. "I mean, I wasn't that broke anyway, I had $500 in the bank. Tramp, pretty independent, you know. I said, 'I'm gonna hang around the crummy all day.' I walked up to the crummy, and I thought, you big punk, they'll be an empty seat on you in the morning. And I stood right there and composed that 'Pursuit of the Silver Strands.' "

With the prolificacy of that other folk poet, Woody Guthrie, Fred has been writing poems ever since. Many are in the meter associated with Robert Service, whom Fred has been accused of copying. Fred replies curtly and accurately, "Robert Service never wrote a logging poem in his life."

Fred is out of the woods now, working on a ranch near Junction City, and I suspect that poems will come from there, too. But I remember Fred Ross best as I first met him, the poet under the hard hat, climbing into his pickup as we waved goodbye, a gesture that for a moment seemed to embrace Oregon itself as we thought of moving East, Fred waving back as he swung the truck in a broad U-turn which for the first time brought a side door into view. On it was painted THE POET OF JUNIPER MOUNTAIN.

10.16.77

17

EXCERPTS FROM NOTEWORTHY STORIES

William Stafford, Northwest Poet
by Rick Rubin
2.6.66

"Talking to him, one finds the conversation turning to one's self or external things, but almost never to Stafford, and should he suspect you of trying to force the conversation around to his life he is likely to surround himself with a convoy of people.

"But what might seem a lack of candor or an excess of modesty in someone else, seems proper in Stafford, for he is a poet, Oregon's most widely acclaimed, and a poet tells of himself best through his poetry, not his conversation."

A Cowpoke Called Reub
by Marjorie O'Hara
5.19.68

"Reub Long, a sagebrush desert rancher whose reputation as a campfire philosopher has traveled as far as his reputation as an Oregon cattleman, paused, grinned, then offered a word of solemn advice:

" 'If I'm going to go on telling you folks stories about this country, I want you to remember just one thing—more than half the darned lies I tell are the honest truth.'

"...'I dreamed once I went to Heaven. St. Paul looked me over more than casually, then he asked, 'Where you from, cowboy?' 'The Fort Rock desert,' I told him. 'Well, all right,' St. Peter said, 'you can come in, but I can tell you right now, you ain't a-goin' to like it, because it ain't a bit like Fort Rock up here.' "

Henk Pander: Why He Paints
by Daniel Yost
12.5.71

"He said there is a strong anti-American sentiment among European intellectuals and that his friends told him he was crazy for wanting to go to such a 'fascist place.' But Henk says he came here and remains, as a more or less permanent immigrant, be-

19

cause 'America is a creative, exciting place with fantastic potential. It is the greatest power in the world, the place where the destruction or salvation of man is going to be settled.' "

Bill Bowerman: He's Not Just Plain Bill
by Leo Davis
6.4.72

"He has been damned as a tyrant and applauded as a genius. He might be neither, he could be both. Bowerman has coached more sub-four milers than any man in history. Detractors insist his protégés run from not for him. He pioneered better shoes, lectured abroad, fought bitterly at home against power monopolies. And been censured for ego trips."

Derroll Adams: Legend of Portland Town
by Irene Schultens
8.20.72

"Derroll Adams [author of 'Portland Town'] became a folk legend to all the young Europeans whose enthusiasm for folk music had gone from just a fad to a real love of the music.

..."At home in Belgium, he has steady club jobs and has time to take it easy and work on new songs...[But] he has learned his lesson to copyright his material from his experience with 'Portland Town,' a song that brought him no money at all. His songs are inseparable from his banjo accompaniment, a very personal simple style of rippling and picking fitting perfectly his low melodic and growling voice.

" 'I have a lot of Oregon in my songs, the wide sky over the Columbia River, the sounds of the freight train that will always be with me, and my strongest memories of Portland, the park blocks down there in front of the museum. I always remember that in autumn time, walking through there, kicking up the leaves and all that—you know. That's all in my song 'The Valley.' The song he refers to is one of the most catching melodies he has played in public, with lines that alone approach sentimentality, but work beautifully as a song. The chorus goes:

"Children's hopes are like green tree leaves
"They soon fade and tumble down
"Come to rest in that lonesome valley
"Where they never can again be found."

Primus St. John—Poet
by Marilyn E. Matteson
9.23.73
" 'I can't take publishing seriously anymore,' he said. 'I can tell that I won't be preoccupied with writing poetry for the rest of my life. The American success ethic can pervert people's interests and intentions, and I want to avoid that....

" 'America is a physically beautiful country, but aspects of its vision are stupid. It refuses to resolve tensions arising from basic contradictions between ideological intentions and actual practices. American history shows it's a country for white people. That can only be so by building a world which estranges others from a healthy situation for growth and development. Because of the basic contradiction, America is continually gnawed at by reality and chooses to see reality as subversive to its ambition. If power must be hooked up with distortion, I'd rather not be powerful.' "

The Governor They Call Tom
by Douglas Seymour
11.4.73
"In his early seven years in office, McCall has met more people personally than any other Oregon governor in history and probably more than any governor in the nation. One reason was the weekly open house in the Capitol which he innovated when he took office...Unlike some governors, McCall doesn't have a regal idea of the role of the chief executive of the state. He abandons the formality often present in governors' offices. When he meets people, informality is the rule."

Memories of Wayne Morse
by Mike Lloyd
8.11.74

"Morse stood, and when the applause subsided and he spoke, I learned two things: Never judge a man by his pinstripes and never stand too close to the loudspeaker when Wayne Morse speaks.

"If there was anything old about him at first, it vanished when he spoke. He was a whirlwind of wrath, an inferno of energy, jabbing an accusing finger at his opponent, calling forth detailed histories of how the country got into Vietnam and why he did and said what he did then. And what he did and said was so true that it hurt to listen to him now and know that no one listened then."

What Ever Happened To Monte Ballou?
by Peter N. Tugman
7.30.78

"Ballou and his Castle Jazz Band probably hit its peak when they played a one night stand in Los Angeles for the Dixieland Jubilee in 1949...A Decca recording was made of the session but Ballou's Castle Jazz Band was the only group featured by itself. A music trade paper of the time exclaimed that 'It was a virtually unknown Portland outfit which stole the show.'

"...if you watch Ballou work, listen to him talk and know something about his personal struggle with alcohol and his long-time work with alcoholics, you begin to realize that some of his philosophy of life is coming through in his work—and in his avocation...Many of his compatriots would wear their 30 years' sobriety like a badge—and pontificate. Not Ballou."

Jerry Turner: Behind the Director's Mask in Ashland
by John A. Armstrong
8.24.80

"As for the experimental theater: 'I bristle at the term, borrowed from science, and I don't think it really applies. It implies you don't know how the play's going to come out. If you're talking about a theater which has very special audiences and tends to explore areas which a conventional theater doesn't…I think we ought to take risks…

"It's so easy for a producing organization to always fall back on the tried and true, and if that happens, then we will ourselves become lazy, and we ultimately will not make the contribution that we're capable of making. There should be at least one element of the theater that is risky."

two:

The Place

"Late Winter on Saddle Mountain"
by Rick Rubin
"Deer and elk observe the trail less than we,
their hoof marks cross and recross the path."

"Let Me Tell You a Little About Living in the Woods"
by Daniel Yost
"I blistered my hands swinging the axe and knelt in the
soft, fragrant moss prying the bark loose as mosquitoes
and flies swarmed about my sweat-caked forehead."

"Antics in the Animal Kingdom"
by Ferris Weddle
"It usually isn't what snakes and other reptiles do
which is considered strange, but what strange
things these unloved creatures make men do."

"Winter Surf"
by Ivan Doig
"There is a myth, which residents of the Pacific Northwest
should arrange to have block-printed in the sky above all the rest of
this country, that winter out here is one long sopping downpour."

When Mt. St. Helens Blew…
"A Race Against Death"
by Charles Gould
"Dark boiling clouds then shot high into the air.
In three or four seconds the mountain disappeared.
We could hear roaring. It got louder."

———————

"I'll Never Go Back"
by Joseph R. Bianco
"As we went over the outer walls, blackened by the heat,
we became enveloped in a huge, steaming cloud. Below
us lay the crater, and beneath it was certainly hell."

LATE WINTER ON SADDLE MOUNTAIN

Rick Rubin

In late February the weather was clear and almost warm, a pleasant interlude among winter rains. We had a day to spare, and had never seen the view from Saddle Mountain, the highest peak in the northernmost Oregon Coast Range. We thought we'd walk up and see what there was to see.

The sky was faultless in Portland; we hoped for good weather toward the coast, but took our rain gear anyway. Predictably, the sunshine ran out just where the highway climbs into the Coast Range. Crossing the mountains we saw snow beside the road and all the distant peaks were white.

The turnoff is sixty-four miles west of Portland, nine miles beyond Elsie on the Sunset Highway. We turned north and drove seven miles up a narrow, winding road edged by shoulders of grass and green moss, pastoral and old-fashioned as a road from another time.

Our luck grew better, just as we came in sight of Saddle Mt. The sun broke through. The mountain comes as a surprise, for the Coast Range around there is generally gentle and rolling, but Saddle Mt. is a big rock outcropping, as steep and jagged as any alp.

We parked in the lot at the bottom, empty that late winter day, where there are campsites and picnic tables.

The trail climbs gently by frequent switchbacks up the south side of the mountain, rising in four miles what seems a couple of thousand feet but is probably less, to the summit at 3283 feet. At first the way is through thick alder groves, bare at that time of year, their white trunks luminous and graceful. Higher, we came to Douglas fir and hemlock, the undergrowth salal and Oregon grape and naked stems of salmonberry.

Now and then we'd look up the steep mountainside, considering climbing straight up a gully or open slope, but the trail is a pleasant one and we were in no great hurry. Deer and elk observe the trail less than we; their hoof marks cross and recross the path. There are jagged ribs of rock and tower-like outcroppings on these slopes; the mountain is small but not entirely tame. We stopped at view points to suck an orange and admire the scenery from split halves of logs placed there for the hiker to sit in comfort.

Halfway up the forest begins to thin out. Winter rains had cut the trail here and there, and we stepped cautiously up a place where run-off had turned the path into a miniature watercourse. Higher still we came to patches of snow that edged the trail and finally covered it, so that we had to slosh through slippery spring snow. Three black-tail deer, bedded for the day on a sunny south slope, eyed us as curiously as we eyed them, then climbed their separate ways.

We looked for elk. We'd heard that there were two herds on the mountain, one of ordinary Roosevelt elk, the other uniquely light-colored animals, labeled albino by some. They are said to be the only such herd in existence. We scanned each open ridge and meadow with our binoculars, but without success.

Above us the summit seemed near. We came out into an open meadow, what we thought the peak to our right, but the trail led left. We followed it down a slope and found ourselves on the saddle that gives the mountain its name. Before us was the main peak, a high bald dome crowned by a fire lookout. From the saddle it was a short steep walk to the summit, across one final snowfield.

On top there were sun and wind and two birds we thought ravens soared glossy black around and around the summit, conferring on some important matter. Unimpressive as the altitude may be, from the peak you can see all of the northwest corner of Oregon if the air is clear.

It was clear that day, and through the glasses we studied

Astoria's forested hills and spotted the Astor Column. We traced the Columbia's slate gray path through green hills to the Pacific, then followed the ribbon of white beaches south to Tillamook head, beyond Seaside.

South of that, toward Neahkahnie Mountain, there are jagged peaks, a whole cluttered block of them, and just beyond the twisting silver ribbon of the Nehalem River flowing to the sea. Further south still there was a mountain chain as snow covered as the high Cascades, sign of a cold winter in these usually mild parts. And back across the valley we saw the Cascades themselves, white stumps of the guardian peaks sliced off by clouds.

Somewhere below we heard the whine of a chain saw, the only man-made sound we heard, and through the glasses we spotted the cut-over ridge and single spar of their high-lead logging show.

The lookout cabin on Saddle Mt. had been boarded up for the winter, but visitors had taken the trouble to bash in the door and break all the encircling windows inside. On every available surface they had written their names and towns, to astound and enlighten the deer and elk who climb here to browse.

The snow still hung deep on the north slopes, and the wind was crisp. We sat against the south wall of the cabin, out of the wind, to eat our sandwiches and soak up sunshine. Directly before us was the finest view of all, range after range of hills and mountains silhouetted against the low winter sun, each one a little hazier than the one before, like a many-layered oriental landscape painting.

The trip down was quicker. We cheated a little, following game trails down ridges where the main trail was too pedestrian, but careful not to break the trail banks. We passed the same three deer we'd seen earlier, plus several others, climbing up to graze. Halfway down we detected movement in a far meadow, and the glasses showed us that we'd spotted our elk.

We hurried further down for a closer look, and finally, at the lowest view point, we sat to study them through the glasses to our hearts content. Their big bodies were palomino in color, their front quarters and heads a rich slate brown, their rump patches light as dry straw. Whether they were the fabled albino elk or simply Roosevelt elk in their local winter coat we could not say, but they were exciting to watch, three of them browsing in a little meadow.

Sunshine mixed with a light drizzle as we descended the last easy stretch of trail. From the parking lot we looked back one last time. There is a steep gully straight up to the high saddle; if one were in a great hurry he might climb up that and save some time, but how much is time saved that way worth? It is only a small mountain, of no great difficulty, but the view is very fine. We drove back down the twisting green-lined road to the highway and hurrying human traffic.

4.10.66

LET ME TELL YOU A LITTLE ABOUT LIVING IN THE WOODS

Daniel Yost

On the bookstore shelf, with the moose or canoe standing out elegantly on the glossed paper cover and the story flowing smoothly over 200 freshly printed pages, it looks easy. The young couple, educated in the city but yearning for something different and elemental, put their philosophical and naturalistic intuitions above inexperience, buy the best equipment and a year's supply of food staples, have a bush pilot or pack horses take them into the heart of the Alaskan wilderness and, against amazing odds, not only survive but prosper in the beautiful, rugged setting of unspoiled nature.

Mary and I are city educated; we like the outdoor world, and the idea of primitive living appeals to us, both for its own sake and for the perspective to be derived on 20th Century urban existence. Like the couple in the book, we have set out to put our love for the earth, sky, water and wildlife into practice.

But you won't find our heroic efforts recorded in a paperback; they fall short of the standard. With the barest and worst of supplies (cheap second-hand stuff) and the help of a battered Volkswagen (which made it to the supermarket once a week before it broke down), we have had two cracks at the relative wilderness. Both times we have listened to common sense, which said, "Come back some other time when you're better prepared."

By "relative" wilderness I mean Rosswood, British Columbia. Listed on every map of B.C. I've seen—on the north tip of Kitsumkalum Lake, 30 miles north of Terrace—Rosswood is not a town but a forested area of 25 square miles which approximately 50 people in widely scattered cabins share with the moose, bear, owls and beaver.

Rosswood was the culmination of a trip I took in the summer of 1968 to find and buy wilderness property. I had keyed my trip ahead of time on Terrace, which is 100 miles from the coast on the main road to Prince Rupert, because I hoped it would be far enough north to have inexpensive wild land in its vicinity and close enough to the sea to have moderate weather.

I know now that you just don't go somewhere and expect to buy land—especially if your funds are meager and your knowledge of the area slim. But I didn't know that then. Without bothering to stop at any real estate office, I drove through Terrace, took the first gravel road heading north and 90 minutes later, listened as a Rosswood settler via a Midwest tornado, the '64 Alaska quake and a house fire in Forest Grove, Oregon, described 40 acres of ground owned by a native (as B.C. Indians are called).

I could get the land cheap, Roy, the rugged individualist American, told me, and it was good fertile ground, all the more valuable with a river on one side and a creek passing through it. It had problems, though, he said—no road at present into it and a 17-acre field that was swampy in part from water backed up by beaver dams. A bulldozer could put in a road in no time, he assured me, and the dams would come out with a few sticks of dynamite. I wondered what would become of the beavers.

That evening, after walking into the place on a trail covered with grizzly and moose tracks and falling instantly in love with the view from the field of snow-capped peaks in every direction, I met the native and made him an offer of $1200. The next day, in Terrace, we made the deal at a lawyer's office.

The following year in May I returned to Rosswood with Mary, my wife of four months, now pregnant. We immediately made friends with the Wackers—Roy, Dotti and their nine children. Their property was just upstream on the Beaver River from ours, and their two-room shack and the bunk house for the older boys were the only buildings on the entire river. They planned a more substantial house for the coming winter—three rounds of large spruce logs were already in place—but first Roy had logs to get out for needed cash.

As a temporary measure, Mary and I moved into an abandoned one-room log cabin two miles from the Wackers that was furnished with a wood heater made out of an oil drum and little else. We were there only a few days when Roy asked me to work for him in the woods. He promised to help us with a log home later, so I set aside my goals for the moment and began limbing fallen trees and wrapping choker cables around the logs.

Spring was incredible. Wild roses bloomed. Butterflies, hummingbirds and woodpeckers were everywhere. Black bears bounded in and out of view. The air was fresh and crisp. Stars, brighter than I ever remembered them, complemented the eerie quiet of night.

Neither of us minded hauling water from a nearby creek or sharing with spiders and flies an outhouse which stood stoutly before the towering, white-faced bulk of Goat Mountain. The old ways, we were discovering, were not as tedious as we'd imagined. Life was simplified, somehow easier on the mind. The conveniences of civilization and the concern for appearance were irrelevant now, almost bewildering and frightening in retrospect.

While I spent the days hopping around in the woods, trying to keep pace with Roy's relentless drive, Mary spent a lot of time reading and, conscious of a Rosswood rumor of a prowling grizzly, rarely wandered far from the cabin. She was not alone, however. Another pregnant lady—Moe, the Wacker's cow—had staked a spot outside a window and didn't appear interested in moving until her calf was born. And then there was the surprise visit from a hummingbird, which zoomed in through the open door and stayed for a frantic 30 minutes before finding the way out.

Mary had no time for reading when we moved closer to the Wackers in June. She had a squirming puppy, purchased at the Terrace dog pound, to train and five perpetual-motion Wacker girls, aged 3 to 10, to entertain, as well as her daily tasks of chopping kindling, baking bread and preparing meals for a woods-weary man.

This cabin was larger and better equipped than the first. It was a spruce log house so old that the cedar shake roof was rotting out, but after Roy skidded it out of the woods with his 'dozer to the riverbank near his family's shack, we fixed it up with the comforts to warm the heart of any modern housewife—of 1850.

We had one propane light, a two-burner propane stove with oven, a wood stove that could double as heater if summer evenings grew chilly, a stool that flushed when you dumped a bucket of water into it, a washtub for bathing and water from the river that was tastier and cleaner than the faucet variety.

Of course, one hole in the roof did leak on our bed one night when it rained; mice did scamper across our blankets, interrupting our dreams (until we were given a cat), and mosquitoes were a daily and nightly torment, but that seemed a fair trade for rush-hour traffic and cement walkways.

Or did it? Maybe little things like mosquitoes added up. Or maybe I got tired of seeing Roy's projects progress and mine stand still, feeling powerless without knowledge and experience to act on my own. Maybe we missed our friends back home. Or maybe, after rushing a neighbor lady in labor (who lived five miles away at the other end of Rosswood) to the hospital, we decided it wouldn't be the best place to live with a winter baby due. Whatever, we succumbed to such feelings and returned to Portland for fall and I enrolled at Portland State University to finish work toward teacher certification.

I never did finish teacher training—the feeling of confinement in the classroom was just too strong and too familiar—but in May I did return to Rosswood, alone, for two weeks to prepare the logs for my cabin.

In this first phase of log cabin building, I had help from Roy. In an area of his land yet to be cleared, he dropped 70 jack pines from eight inches to a foot thick with his power saw and cut them into 40-foot lengths. This task took him an hour and a half; mine, limbing and peeling the bark off with an axe, kept me busy for the next 10 days.

Light jogging through city streets had hardly prepared me

for this kind of work, which shamed strawberry picking for its backbreaking propensity and required wrist and arm strength I had to develop along the way. I blistered my hands swinging the axe and knelt in the soft, fragrant moss prying the bark loose as mosquitoes and flies swarmed about my sweat-caked forehead. But it was worth it when I could stop, stretch my body erect, listen to the ravens screaming overhead and the nearby woodpecker methodically poking for his lunch, and survey the random lay of beautiful white pine logs glistening in the sun.

One afternoon a stranger, a lean, powerfully built man with bushy black eyebrows and an ageless, wrinkled face, interrupted my work.

"You must be Pete," I said hesitantly, remembering that Roy had told me of a trapper who was interested in giving me a hand with my cabin.

"Yes," he slurred, revealing the subtlest of grins and a twinkle in his eye. "How long it take you to do one of them logs?"

"Oh, about a half hour if I work at it," I said, wondering if that was too slow.

"You do all this?" he asked, looking over the logs.

"Yes."

"Not bad for a greenhorn," he came back, again with a hint of a grin and the slightest raising of those incredible eyebrows.

Pete was a faller turned wanderer, who worked when the spirit moved him or someone needed help. Now, apparently, the spirit was moving him—I couldn't understand why ("I need the experience," he said)—and he asked only for enough money to pay his expenses.

I remained skeptical, but when I returned to Rosswood in August, after calling Terrace from Portland and securing the job as bus driver for Rosswood's school children, Pete, with the help of two of Roy's older boys, already had several rounds of pine logs up.

It was a great sight, that beginning of a log house sitting there three feet off the ground on cedar posts, about 60 feet from the slow-moving river, and eight-tenths of a mile down a rutted dirt road Roy had pushed out with his bulldozer.

"Two more weeks," Pete said, "and you can move in," and I looked forward to having Mary and Colin, our infant son, join me in our new home.

For the next week I worked with Pete and Tim, 15, at getting the remainder of the basic-frame logs in place. We accomplished this by lifting and pushing them up if they were light enough and winching them up with a tractor if they were too heavy.

Pete was alternately funny and angry in the course of this strenuous and sometimes precarious work.

"This is the way they do it in Siberia," he grinned as we lifted a heavy log off the ground, but a moment later he was yelling, "No, not that way, Stupid," or, "What's the matter, you weak or something?" at Tim or me as we either misunderstood his half-muttered directions or failed to match his incredible strength. (His rage, though, always had an amazingly short lifespan; a moment after he would be making a wry comment or singing one of his corny, sentimental love songs.)

The work didn't go as fast as expected, however. The tractor suffered a broken axle when a front wheel slammed into a stump; Pete's saw (used for notching, trimming and cutting logs to size) was out of order for a couple of days, and intermittent rain cut into work time. At the end of two weeks, Pete had to move on and we had only gotten as far as finishing the rafters.

I was left to my own resources, and I puttered around a few days, digging a hole for a septic tank (I planned to have a toilet and tub that at least drained) and stuffing fiberglass in the cracks between logs.

This work was not particularly enjoyable in itself, but I liked the feeling of being alone in the woods with these tasks, as I had earlier in peeling the logs. The presence of wildlife was the main attraction in this, I think. Crows, ravens and geese seemed always overhead.

A friendly weasel scampered around in a pile of scrap lumber, often stopping to observe my progress. A black bear climbed high on a log pile across the river, raised his head, got a whiff of me and lumbered back into the forest. A snow owl looked blankly at me from a nearby tree. Three moose simultaneously plunged into the river 100 yards downstream from the house, sending a tremendous splash resounding through the valley amphitheater, swam across, climbed up on the bank, paused to shake off some of the water and loped into the dense cover.

I felt a part of this life, at home with it; yet I was lonely for my family. After passing my chauffeur's test in Terrace and learning that it would be at least two weeks before my licence (Canadian spelling) was issued, I drove south to get Mary and Colin.

We returned north to find that Roy had found several large cedar butts for shake wood and that he had even split a few with a hand shake froe and started the roof on one side. That was all he had time for, however (except for the following Sunday when he helped me with the flooring and windows), so the rest was left to me.

As a temporary measure we moved into the cabin near Roy's house (his large, three-story log home was nearing completion), which we had previously occupied. Fall was in the air now. Moose tracks appeared with increasing regularity on the road downriver to our cabin site. Wolves sent plaintive cries skyward at night. And best of all, setting the scene for the winter ahead, numerous owls set the sun to rest and kept up their chorus of mellow hoots through the night.

The excitement, spiced with fear, of the idea of winter, was now a constant preoccupation for us in our work. Mary, with the better part of her time taken up with a crawling boy, hurried in free moments to keep the wood stove stoked and baked bread, some of which we traded to a neighbor for milk. And meanwhile, I set to work overcoming my doubts and inexperience.

Without the use of Roy's chain saw (which, like Pete's, had bitten too much sawdust), the job of sawing the bulky cedar butts into two-foot lengths by hand was an enormous job. The rest of the work—splitting the wood, making shakes and then nailing them up—was time-consuming but enjoyable.

A week later, after trial and error and sweat and strain and blackfly bites, I was perched on the ridge pole nailing up the last few shakes while Mary, with Colin in a backpack, was below picking rose hips for jam in our own private wild rose patch. I had feelings of relief and triumph in getting that colorful, fragrant roof on. I also felt that, in a small way, I had carried on with the family building tradition. My grandfather, a carpenter and contractor, had his houses, bridges and the Oregon City elevator. My father had his four-bedroom home with full basement. I had a 16-by-24 log cabin.

But the work was not yet done by any means. And now my job driving the school bus took me away from Rosswood during the day. Throughout October I worked on the house on weekends and sometimes in the evening, building a stairway to the upstairs, a woodshed on one end of the house, stapling insulation on the inside of the roof and putting a partition between the kitchen and bathroom. I found a used stool and tub for a few dollars, and Roy helped me hook them up while also cutting half-inch spruce boards on his own portable sawmill for the inside of the roof.

By the second week in November we were ready to move in. With the tub, three propane lights and a good wood heater to go with the wood cook stove, it was another step upward in comfort in Rosswood living. But with considerable inside work yet to do—shelves, more insulating, plastic reinforcing to go over windows—and daily woodcutting as well—there was no time to sit back and enjoy our new home.

Woodcutting, unfortunately, had been left to the last minute each day. With the air cooling, we had our cabin up, but no winter's supply of firewood neatly stacked in the woodshed. For the moment, at least, this seemed only a minor problem. We had plenty of small alder trees—now bare of leaves—outside our cabin and it was only a matter of a half hour or so of swinging with my trusty axe to fill our wood box for another day.

By this means, I hoped to make it until Christmas vacation. The temperature, for a week in the dead of winter, had been known to hit 30 below in Rosswood. Roy said it was imperative in such cold times to have birch logs, which gave off considerably more heat than the green alder I was using, for firewood.

With Roy's help, and assistance from other neighbors, I planned to make good use of the coming vacation to get an adequate supply of birch.

We never made it to Christmas vacation. The cold days this winter came, not in January or February, but a few days into December. In short order, the thermometer registered zero as six inches of powder snow fell. Then it hit 10, and 20 below. The wind howled off the lake, rattling our roof and blowing icy air through cracks around the door I couldn't seem to seal up. The floor was cold, too, because I had yet to plug all the cracks around the cedar posts which held our house off the ground.

The worst of it was that I still had to leave during the day to drive the school children into town. One afternoon I came home to find water left in the bath tub frozen and Mary and Colin, heavily clothed, huddling near the heater.

I hurriedly gulped down a little food and then went outside, with my feet icing up in leather boots, to chop for water through eight inches of ice on our side of the river and chop for wood through alder logs hard as metal from frozen pitch.

Mary wasn't complaining, nor was Colin with his cheeks a sickly red. But it was just too cold that day, and that night. We quickly made the decision to leave for a warmer climate (Portland seemed like Miami Beach when we returned here after hitting a low of 45 below driving through Prince George) and come back some other time, wiser for the experience and more prepared to cope with the realities.

So now the cabin sits there at the end of a road used by the moose. Its windows are boarded up; grass is growing tall in the rich soil around it, and its own house guests are mice. When we will occupy it again, I don't know. It deserves to be more than a vacation home. Maybe when city air becomes intolerable. Maybe when I figure out how the couple in the paperback does it.

11.14.71

ANTICS IN THE ANIMAL KINGDOM

Ferris Weddle

Two woodsmen were traveling in a jeep on a back-country road in Idaho when they spied a deer fawn racing across a clearing. The fawn was obviously terrified, and curious about the cause, the driver halted his vehicle.

The young deer did not hesitate when it saw the jeep. Veering slightly, it dashed to the vehicle, and leaped into the backseat. There, under the flabbergasted stares of the men, it flopped down, panting. Fresh blood oozed from several scratches on the fawn's shoulders and flanks, so the men assumed the animal had had a close call with either a bobcat or a cougar.

Since no pursuer appeared, the men tried to persuade the fawn to leave its temporary refuge. The fawn refused to leave with a finality that left no doubt that it figured it had found a very safe place! Resigned, the driver took the fawn home with him where it was welcomed by the family. After a few days rest, its wounds healed, the fawn departed for its wilderness world.

The above is only one of numerous anecdotes I've collected through the years involving mankind and other members of the animal kingdom. Some of the true antics border on the "tall tales" told around campfires. In some cases, man is the instigator, or the reason for the antics, but in many instances wild mammals, birds, or other creatures get out of the rut where mankind has shoved them.

Apparently hitch-hiking deer aren't so rare. In Oklahoma, a minister heard a terrific noise in his trailer shortly after he had left a wildlife refuge. The minister investigated and found a deer had taken refuge in the trailer. Well, outside the refuge the deer season was open, so no doubt you can guess the outcome.

A Colorado hunter had a different kind of hitchhiker—a dead one, he thought. He knocked over a cougar with his auto on a highway and since the cougar appeared dead, he loaded the cat into the car's trunk.

Later, opening the trunk to show his catch to a game warden for the bounty then being paid in Colorado on cougars, the man was somewhat taken aback when he faced a snarling, very alive cougar. He sensibly slammed the trunk shut and with help managed to dispatch the feline with a rifle.

A South Dakota woman had a stowaway, too. While driving from her ranch to a nearby town, she kept hearing strange sounds from under her vehicle's hood. Finally, the engine stopped altogether and the irate woman lifted the hood to see if she could locate the problem.

She located it all right—a very large, very hot and very angry raccoon! In its efforts to escape, it had torn loose varied and sundry wires, and now with freedom at hand, it wasted no time in taking off. The woman had to hitch a ride into town to get the aid of a repairman.

Quite frequently, no doubt accidentally most of the time, animals help one another. There was the case of a whitetail deer in Nebraska which was trapped in a mesh net corral for transplanting purposes. The deer escaped because, for reasons unknown, a jack rabbit chewed a hole in the netting.

An Idaho pheasant rooster apparently knew exactly what he was doing. A cat was seen crouched in the grass, ready to spring on an unsuspecting pheasant hen. The rooster let loose a squawk and landed on top of the cat. By the time the pheasant was through pecking, and beating the feline with its wings, the cat was only too happy to escape.

It seems, too, that pheasants—and other birds—are practically brotherhood; or perhaps they're trying the commune system. At any rate, a pheasant hen laid her eggs in a nest occupied by a domestic hen. No doubt the latter figured the world population had truly exploded—she was already uncomplainingly brooding some eggs deposited by a mallard duck.

It usually isn't what snakes and other reptiles do which is considered strange, but what strange things these unloved creatures make men do. My favorite snake story concerns an amateur woodsman hunting in New Mexico. The man found and killed an unusually large rattlesnake just outside his tent. That night, in his bedroll, he began thinking about keeping the rattles as a souvenir.

Fearing some animal might drag the snake off in the night, he got up, and in the semi-darkness he grabbed up the snake and whacked off its rattles. The next morning he observed a fearsome sight. The rattler he had killed earlier lay where he had tossed it—its rattles still much intact. And meandering through the dust and grass was the bloody trail of a serpent that would likely never again indulge in traditional rattling!

Snakes, of course, occasionally do silly things, too. There was a Texas bullsnake, for instance, which swallowed a soft drink bottle.

It might be somewhat soothing for mankind, irked and disgusted with human follies, to reflect on the antics of animals in the sometimes zany merry-go-round that is life.

11.27.66

45

WINTER SURF

Ivan Doig

I suppose I've made the usual journeys to the edges of myself. The grain truck that wrenched itself apart and skidded brokenly for what seemed like a week carried me as far as I want to go into danger and fear.

The love trip has been with that best of all possible traveling companions, a working wife.

Despondency. The thrill, a time or maybe two, of doing the best work I am capable of. Anger. Stupidity. One way or another, they've all turned up on the itinerary.

One journey, however, I make time and again, on foot and as free and light as I ever am. This is the trip to the edge of myself that is also the edge of the land world—to the exhilaration of the winter ocean.

We came up and out of the sea, evolutions ago. Perhaps those beginnings account for tuggings toward the water. Oceans roll in from the springs of time, somewhere; the pulse of the surf may be speaking directly to the rhythms the human body lives by.

What accounts for my own feeling for the ocean shore in the gray winter weather, I'm not entirely sure. Many things, maybe. But probably somewhere in there is a snobbish satisfaction in having to one's self a world the rest of humanity considers out of season.

There is a myth, which residents of the Pacific Northwest should arrange to have block-printed in the sky above all the rest of this country, that winter out here is one long sopping downpour.

Yes, it rains. But the winter hiker knows two secrets about the Northwest rain which nobody else seems to grasp.

One, it doesn't rain that much.

Two, it doesn't matter a whole lot if it does.

Take secret number two first of all. Not many people realize it, but we are the heirs of a revolution started more than a century ago by a Scotsman named Charles Macintosh.

Mac invented a raincoat made of rubberized cloth. By way of some versions which were like wearing a very large hot water bottle, we now have light, ventilated, rainproof jackets and pants.

When the 25th century looks back on our civilization, these rain clothes will be the sole evidence that we ever made any progress at all.

To return to the first secret: The sun does shine in winter, sometimes. I've seen the wings of snow geese flash white in the sunshine above Skagit Bay, for instance. Even the weather along the Pacific shore can be bright, with a low field of clouds far out to herald the coming of another low pressure system.

Catching the sun in winter is a matter of staying alert, especially if you get out only on weekends. You keep your hiking gear ready to go, and if the day shows any sign at all of being clear, you use it. You never wait to see if the next day will be better, because tomorrow comes the deluge.

But again, the deluge has more to be said for it than most people suspect. The walker under clouds or rain can experience a deep mood which the exuberance of sunshine rarely offers.

Take this instance: Damp winter is the best time to see nature reclaiming a deserted homestead.

On the Olympic Peninsula, in an area where no roads have been built to the beach, you come across the westernmost homestead in the lower 48 states. Lars Ahlstrom, who lived alone out here on the end of the continent, died in 1960.

For several years, my wife and I have gone there periodically, watching the forest and high grass take back the clearing. Standing in the permanent squish of the path in a winter drizzle, we think man's hold on the land is slight, slight.

Also, in winter you meet persons who devoutly prize the outdoors. Once, tired and dripping from a backpack trip along the shore rocks in the rain, we searched out a shelter where we could savor a fire and hot tea. The one we found had a fire already roaring, with a young couple snuggled close. They happily invited us in and fed us.

Glancing around, we noticed that the crude shelter was jammed with camping gear and food. Yes, the couple said, they had been there a week or so, and would stay another week or more. They were on their honeymoon.

I suspect there may be an ultimate reason, beyond even honeymoons and homesteads, to seek the sea hem of this land.

For perhaps, maybe even probably, we will choke this planet to death with our filth and garbage, and along the way life will become a husk of the earth's best offering now.

That may be the deepest reason for booted journeys across the damp sand and rock towards the edge of the self. Man's words never convey life's tone precisely enough; I prefer the elegies pounded out exhilaratingly by the surf in the winter afternoon.

12.6.70

A RACE AGAINST DEATH

Charles Gould

D on LaPlaunt, 45, knows the area like the palm of his hand. The Chehalis, Wash., resident has spent as many as three months at a stretch in those woods during deer and goat hunting season, hunting with bow and rifle. He knows the very best fishing holes, too.

Don also knows a secluded spot just below Green River that offered the most spectacular view of Mount St. Helens. On Mother's Day (May 11) he camped there with his family and they witnessed "30 minor eruptions on the mountain in a four-hour period." Don, a divorced father of five, wanted to show the campsite with the spectacular view to his friends, newly arrived from Wisconsin, Lynn Westlund and his wife Julie, now residents of Packwood, near Mount Rainier. Lynn is the brother of Don's girlfriend, Kathy Pearson.

Late Saturday (May 17), Don LaPlaunt took Kathy, his two youngest sons, Daniel, 17, and David, 13, and the Westlunds on an overnight camp-out. The Westlunds, in their pickup, followed the LaPlaunt Chevy up a zigzagging logging road. On the way up, they startled a bobcat. They arrived at the camp around midnight, unloaded their camping gear, and turned in.

It was peaceful and clear. Mount St. Helens could be seen in the distance standing quietly in the near darkness. A herd of elk grazed in the meadow around them. So far the weather report was right; it seemed Sunday would after all be a day of cloudless blue sky.

The boys slept in the car; the Westlunds slept on the bed of their pickup under a canopy; and Don and Kathy bedded down under the bright stars.

LaPlaunt did not select the camp frivolously. Reports of the mountain's activity and the possibility of a major eruption were taken into serious consideration. They were five miles outside the "Red Zone" with a "direct exit north."

Shortly after 8 a.m. Don awakened. He didn't get up right away. He lay looking at the mountains under a sky glowing with sunshine and barely a trace of cloud. It looked close enough to touch.

Around 8:30, the pickup and the car shook. It startled the LaPlaunt boys and the Westlunds. Curiously, Kathy and Don, lying on the ground, did not feel the quake. A few seconds later, Don pointed to a "puff of smoke" rising from the mountain. At first it looked similar to the many minor eruptions he had seen a week before.

"I had a perfect view," Don said. "The whole mountain could be seen through a saddle in the ridge. As it started out, everybody had a smile on their faces to see another eruption."

Then they saw the explosion! "At first," Don said, "it was shaped like a baseball, and then it broadened at the bottom, quickly." He stretched his cupped hands apart in front of him as though he were describing a large fish. "Dark boiling clouds then shot high into the air. In three or four seconds the mountain disappeared. We could hear roaring. It got louder."

They noticed the cloud advancing furiously in their direction. The ridge in front of them was about five miles away, half way between them and the mountain. "I saw a shock wave blast through the ridge miles to the left of us and then to the right," Don said. "Then and there I could see how enormous it was. It uprooted trees like they were nothing. And then it loomed over the ridge in front of us like a mile-high tidal wave. It was turbulent, churning in every direction—it engulfed everything as it came. It only took that wave 30 seconds to reach the ridge! It must have traveled 500 miles an hour!"

Don yelled, "Oh my God! Run! Leave everything!"

They responded speedily. The Westlunds abandoned their pickup and all their expensive camping equipment. Lynn left his new pistol and a $60 hunting knife. Don grabbed his pistol but couldn't remember taking it, or why. They all jumped into the car, Kathy without her boots, Daniel without his pants. Daniel took pictures out the window as they sped away.

With Don at the wheel the car raced down the gravelly logging road with the mountain in hot pursuit. Don floorboarded the '69 Chevy Impala. As they shot down the hill, Lynn said he could feel heat on the back of his head. Daniel and David checked the speedometer and saw that their father was doing 60 mph down a mountain road full of hairpin curves. "I had one thing on my mind," Don said, "to get as far away as fast as I could. I know I flew over holes in the road and went over limbs six inches through. I couldn't have gone too fast to suit anybody. Kathy thought I was going to have a heart attack because I was breathing hard and fast and gritting my teeth. I was scared; I had seen something."

"We met only one car on the way down," Daniel said. "It was a pickup and it had two guys sitting in the back in a boat. We told them to get out."

"I have no idea what happened to them," Don said with a look that gave scant hope.

A little farther down they passed an occupied campsite. Don turned back. A few people were around a campfire. They had a camper and a tent. They didn't know yet what had occurred. A woman in the group wanted to question them further about what was happening.

"The mountain's blown!" Don yelled. "Get out! You have no time to waste!"

By this time, winds of hurricane force had caught up with the fleeing car. Don had all the vents closed. "It was getting darker by the minute," he said. "Anybody have any prayers to say, say them now. We knew we had had it—written ourselves off. Lightning was flashing all around us—heat lightning."

David said, "There was a noise like thunder under ground."

"I didn't think anything was going to be left," Don said. "I thought for sure the whole world was engulfed." But luck was with them. "For the next couple of miles we drove through a logged-out area. Had there been standing trees we'd have had it. And when we neared Riffe Lake there was a tremendous up-draft that kept the worst part of the turbulence above us. And that's what saved us," Don said.

But they still were surrounded with darkness, noise and turmoil. When they descended to the east end of Riffe Lake, they saw several campers standing outside their cabins drinking coffee. "We warned them," Don said. "Oh, we know it," said one woman, as though there were nothing to worry about. The Chevy continued in full flight.

Don estimated they had traveled 15 miles down the mountain to Riffe Lake in less than 20 minutes.

More turbulence hit them as they approached U.S. 12. "Big old mud balls, the size of my thumb," pelted the car, said Don. He grabbed the closest thing at hand to wipe off the windshield; it was underwear. He reached out while driving to clear a spot he could barely see through. When they finally reached U.S. 12, the mud had turned to ash and was falling heavily.

They turned northwest and drove through the falling ash to the little logging town of Morton. There was a quarter of an inch there already. They debated in Morton whether to drive north to Tacoma or west to Chehalis and home. They turned west where they saw a bright spot in the sky.

When they reached Onalaska, they stopped at a friend's house for 20 minutes, had coffee and called friends and relatives. They entered Chehalis a little after 10 a.m., 1½ hours after the mountain had blown its top. "The boys were still shaking," said Isabel LaPlaunt, Don's mother.

They had witnessed the most colossal explosive force on this continent within the living memory of man. And they had survived.

In the safety and comfort of his home, with his mother and his two young boys on hand, Don looked back on their narrow escape. "I know for a fact that within 45 seconds of the blast on the mountain our camp was destroyed. If we'd stayed there one or two seconds more we would not be here now. I've seen pictures of the Green River area and most of the timber is flat—

the pickups and cars, buried. Dust engulfed everything. I know now what it must have felt like in Hiroshima. I honestly thought we'd be safe 10 miles from the mountain—I heard people were killed 30 miles away." Then with solemnity and gratitude, he said, "We thank somebody else besides ourselves for getting us out of there."

Kathy Pearson is still shaken by the experience, said Don. Kathy works for the Forest Service in Packwood 40 miles northwest of Mount St. Helens and about 20 miles south of Mount Rainier. Near her home is a crater lake. She has often, as part of her job, accompanied work crews in the blast area. One tree planting crew out of Packwood was killed. Kathy has nightmares about her experience, said Don.

The boys, over their fright, joke about their run against death. "Thank you, Diehard," they say.

Don LaPlaunt is back to work as a millwright foreman at the Satsop Nuclear Plant in Elma. He still thinks a lot about what happened to him and those with him. He thinks about friends and acquaintances lost and others unaccounted for. And after all this the mountain still draws him.

"I can't wait for the opportunity to go back up there," Don said, "to see what happened to the area we were in. I know I won't recognize it. Probably won't even be able to find it. I knew the whole area around that mountain. When we left Saturday, I could have gone to terrific campsites east, west, or south of the mountain." Then Don shook his head. "But I went to the north side. If there was gonna be any action on Mount St. Helens, that's where I wanted to be. Got more than I bargained for."

6.1.80

I'LL NEVER GO BACK

Joseph R. Bianco

About 45 miles north of the most livable city in the United States is hell.

I know. I saw it. And it scared the living daylights out of me.

What they said about our mountain is only half of it. The other half has to be seen to realize what happened up there. And when you have seen it, as I have, you still can't believe it. There is only one thing I may have on the person who hasn't seen the volcano, and that is I saw what death must be like and returned.

They tell us there may be a national park there some day or some other tourist attraction. I don't care what they have. I'm not going back.

Mount St. Helens to me doesn't exist. To me, the "saint" that was is now Satan. No saint would ever turn paradise into hell.

I wanted to see the volcano before I believed it was necessary to see it. I had been working on a project with writers and photographers who had seen the mountain.

To get a better understanding, I had to go. I'm not sorry I went. But I don't know whether I'll enjoy remembering it. I don't like the color gray.

Today, Mount St. Helens is gray. It's what some may call an ashen gray. It's the color that comes across a person's face when he dies. I've seen death before. Now I've seen Mount St. Helens. Can there be worse?

I saw photographs before I went up there. Almost everybody has. I was shocked, as everyone was. But now I was actually there. Fortunately, the pilot of the helicopter had briefed us and his tone was such to allay any fears. However, I expected some shock.

The helicopter passed over some unaffected areas before its journey into the destructive zone. The green lush landscape, familiar to me, was soothing. I waited calmly and readied my cameras.

Without any warning, I suddenly became aware that we were there or approaching within view. There was a quiet in the aircraft except for the deafening chatter of the chopper blades. I looked out of the porthole and saw it. I had to get a better look. The entry hatch was opened like a Dutch door for the convenience of photographers. I looked and stared and then took some photographs. I looked some more and then put my camera aside. I stared below as the aircraft moved slowly across the gray, dead hills of the Toutle River Valley.

"My God," I said. "Why?"

Down there beneath tons of ash and rock and broken trees had been life. Vegetative and human. Now there was none.

You just don't fly over and not do anything. I remembered before boarding the aircraft I saw a small, frail woman in her 70s holding a wreath made of daisies. She was no taller than my mother. She had wanted to go along with us. But the Army said no.

I said a prayer for her because I felt she had apparently lost someone up there. I said a prayer for others who also were victims of that Sunday morning holocaust.

You can take pictures of the destruction. You can hear reports from survey teams and others whose business it is to search and bring back the dead. But you never can feel the impact of that scene up there unless you see it. Then, and even then, it is hard to believe how destructive nature can be. Nature gave it to us and took it away in one swoop.

When I had to be told "that was Spirit Lake," I knew then it would be difficult to describe the disfiguration and ugliness of what was once the most beautiful lake in all the forests.

Tons and tons of fallen timber gray with ash lay still on a dead lake. The lake had been almost covered by the blown timber, fallen rocks and ice. Some water, however, still was visible in small, steaming pools.

And the gray hills surrounding the lake, stripped of all standing timber, seemed more like rows of giant tombstones marking the place where Spirit Lake had been.

It was hard to believe the reports of the power of that May 18 eruption. Now that I've seen the force of the evil of that volcano, it is not hard to accept some of the stories that are coming back from the searchers who discovered the dead.

A member of a search party told me he came upon one victim who was literally fried by the heat and tried to claw his way through the windshield. His hands were distorted and shaped like claws. His eyes were hanging from their sockets. There were many more stories, equally gruesome.

The horror below doesn't stop. There is more than one wants to see. It's a mass of all gray moguls in places and curving crevices whose walls are colored a sickening brown.

As we were approaching the summit near the outer walls of the two-mile-long crater, the pilot motioned me forward to the cockpit and told me we were going in.

"Do we have to?" were the only words which came out of my mouth. He smiled, nodded his head because he couldn't hear me, and pointed ahead.

As we went over the outer walls, blackened by the heat, we became enveloped in a huge, steaming cloud. Below us lay the crater, and beneath it was certainly hell.

My only thought was: "Let's get out of here."

The aircraft was out of the cloud within minutes and soon, but not fast enough for me, we were on the south side of the volcano, away from the treacherous north side. Little did we know then that the puff of steam was the beginning of a small eruption clocked at 2:30 p.m. to be followed by another major eruption nine hours later at 11:30 p.m. May 25, when volcanic ash drifted southward to our most livable city, Portland.

As we left the south face, we circled the volcano for our

journey back. It was raining hard and it was cold and the clouds swirled ominously above us. Suddenly, there was excitement aboard the aircraft. A small green pickup was spotted resting upright on a logging road. The panels had been caved in. The cab of the truck was opened. A piece of clothing was stuck in the door jamb and was flapping in the mountain wind almost as if someone had placed it there calling for help. There was no way anyone there could have helped. It was only three or four miles from the center of the blast. There was no sign of the driver.

We hovered for a few minutes. We were certain no dead were in there. If they did get out, they were only a few feet away, buried in the avalanche of ash and mud.

The aircraft now banked and headed for the base of Toledo. At least that was what I was hoping for. You can stay up there for hours, even for days, if it were possible, photographing everything in sight, but you can not bring back in either words or pictures what happened that Sunday morning in May.

Finally, the aircraft entered the stretches of green timber and we came back to reality again. Below us was the Gifford Pinchot National Forest the way many of us knew it. As the aircraft landed, I knew that while we were away for only an hour or so, what we saw would be with us for the rest of our lives. And I'm sure the people who live within view of Mount St. Helens, the volcano, will be thinking of the beauty who had gone mad and changed their lives and the lives of others who came within our reach.

It was then I thought about that little old lady who wanted to go with us. As we got off the aircraft and headed for the briefing area, I saw her again. She was still there holding the wreath. She wasn't going to give up. She planned to get that wreath out there somehow. She looked determined. Her brother was out there, she told me. She loved him very much. And I know Harry Truman must have loved her, too.

(Many readers will recall that Harry Truman was the spunky resident who refused to evacuate the mountain.)

6.1.80

EXCERPTS FROM NOTEWORTHY STORIES

Our Mountain
by John Clark Hunt
6.11.67

"There are a hundred reasons why we love a mountain or all mountains and why tens of thousands, perhaps hundreds of thousands, of people think first of Mt. Hood when mountains are mentioned. Some say they love it because it is the almost perfect mountain—the great green and white pyramid outlined against the sky.

"Hood and its fellows have dominated the view of man each time he lifted his eyes to the heavens in this region. Ages ago the Indians called it Wyeast. A British Naval Officer, Lt. Broughton, while exploring the lower Columbia in October 1792 named it Hood to honor his Admiral. From time to time Americans have wanted to change the name to something American but it was firmly fixed on our maps and in Western history and literature as Hood."

'Squippies' in the Outback of Oregon
by David Shetzline
11.23.69

"The Oregonian is an odd one about his artists, though. He stocks his library with western history, trail guides, Oregon lore. Yet too often finds little space for his own novelists, who make much more profound sense of the Oregon experience than any camp manual or photograph collection. And upon his walls hang excellent craft but not much of the more complex, extraordinary work northwest painters can produce. It is as if Oregonians are infatuated with their landscapes and seek works in accord, works blending with the countenance of Mount Hood.

"...Americans are coming. In the next generation they will seek more and more of what we have here, in the Oregon Preserve, the Territory Ahead. If under these pressures we are to accommodate them, we must take greater care of our own artists, our own dissenters. We must attend those who would make great monuments of our style, our special Oregon lore, our individual secrets, our beauty. Mount Hood will not be enough."

(Squippies, a takeoff on hippies, is the author's term for bohemians who live in the damp outback.)

The Seven Wonders of Oregon
by Cecil M. Ouellette
3.31.74

1. Crater Lake…"Looking out over this spectacle of space, light, lake and silence from the big, breezy rim of the caldera, you may be inclined to believe that this is the bluest and purest place on earth."

2. The Willamette River…"This is a big, beautiful river—its surface ever-changing, its moods varied and intriguing, and the outdoor experiences along its 200-some miles are as many as one cares to make them."

3. Mt. Hood…"that great alabaster tower in the sky that sometimes floats cloudlike on the horizon, sometimes looming sharp and clear after a storm"

4. The Columbia River Gorge…"a monument imbedded in stone"

5. John Day Fossil Beds…"30 million years of earth history are laid open like a book from bedrock to rim."

6. The Oregon Dunes…"a superb sand wilderness of desertlike dunes, evershifting and drifting to the timeless tune of the wind"

7. The Wallowas…"a match for the mountains of Switzerland or Austria."

three:
Issues & Concerns

The Environment:
"Man: The Marvelous Pollution Machine"
by Art Chenoweth
" *'In this society10 years is a long range plan. Planning
should be in hundreds of years, not 10s of years.'   "*

———————

" 'Let's Clear the Air…': The Fight To Save Our Home"
by Barry Lopez
*"We have been run over, as if by a truck. We are intimidated
and browbeaten by sudden, self-proclaimed experts,
lectured to by bandwagon politicians, pacified by
misleading advertising and left, in the end, confused."*

Personal Liberties: Are We Losing Our Freedoms?
"Ursula Le Guin—It's Time To Decentralize"
by Daniel Yost
*"We all know we're imprisoned by things, money, by buying and
selling. And I think when we realize what the priorities really are…"*

———————

"Mike Russo—It Doesn't Look Hopeful"
by Daniel Yost
*"I think what we need in our country is a very powerful
independent force which, if it didn't win the election, at least
could exercise an enormous influence and pressure for change."*

———————

"Let's Not Overreact"
by Larry Leonard
*"If bombings bother you, you're normal. If they make
you mad, you are part of the establishment..."*

The Changing Family:
"Is the Family Becoming Extinct?"
by Art Chenoweth
*"By now, as we all know from experience, the family has lost
to the state all its political functions, most of its economic
functions and almost all of its educational functions."*

———————

"Who Are These People?"
by Paul Pintarich
*"Where in early rural America families lived together for
generations, now we have the departure of the young.
Each to his own and no more additions to the family
home when the son or daughter marries."*

MAN: THE MARVELOUS POLLUTION MACHINE

Art Chenoweth

M an is a polluter by nature. He has been making his world a garbage dump since his time began. Even now, when he sees he may be polluting himself into extinction, he continues to spread his offal in and around the world.

Is there a solution for man, the natural dumper? Yes, possibly (it may be too late) but the solution is not an easy one. It will require a complete change in some of our most basic ways of looking at things.

Among the scientists who have been worrying and speculating about pollution and its dangers to survival are the anthropologists, the men who examine the origin, development, races, customs and beliefs of mankind.

One of Oregon's leading anthropologists, Dr. Wilbur A. (Buck) Davis, head of the anthropology department at Oregon State University, explained how man got himself into this pickle.

Even considered as an animal, man is far different from any of his fellow animals. He is the widest ranging, from the equator almost to the poles. He is a manipulator of his environment—he manipulates it and exploits it as much as possible.

He is a cultural animal. He adapts to his natural environment by modifying it, so that he can exist in almost any habitat or ecological zone.

Animals also modify their environments to a limited extent, through the construction of burrows or nests. Man does it through utilization of raw materials and the manufacture of very complex material objects. In this way, he creates shelter, protection from the elements, subsistence.

However, during this process of manufacture, there is always a certain amount of wastage—"debitage" as Dr. Davis calls it. Heretofore, the waste has simply been discarded.

In simple societies, the people just throw things on the ground. This practice continues through the more advanced civilizations and into the industrial age today.

This does have one value. Littering is a boon to the study of archaeology. You can learn much about a vanished civilization by its refuse.

In the leavings of the past, archaeologists find tools, and tools to make tools. They collect products all through the range of manufacture, from design to finished implement. They can access the range of skills, the availability and use of materials and many of the cultural values of bygone civilizations.

Visualize what future archaeologists may deduce about our civilization by the stacks of beer cans along the roads. The cans will be there. A beer can thrown by Columbus would still be a beer can today.

Naturally, in past times, there have been instances where the stuff accumulated on the ground to the point where it became burdensome. You could smell it, or you kept tripping over it.

"If you didn't mind the smell," said Dr. Davis, "You let it accumulate; if you did, you swept it out."

He recalled the story of the Montana cowboy in the remote log cabin. Visitors complained that litter in the cabin was getting mighty deep.

"Well," said the cowboy, "I figure you can only keep trackin' it in so long and then you start trackin' it back out again." So, from the simplest hunting and gathering societies, up through the agricultural or food producing societies, man has maintained a casual attitude about his waste. It is simply a matter of convenience as to where you disposed it.

"This casual attitude is basic to our present problem," said Dr. Davis. "At no time in the past have societies stopped to consider the long-range problems of waste disposal. Dealing with pollutants has been a matter of expediency. Usually the easy way is just to cover it up."

This is why some of the ancient cities of the East are built on huge mounds. These mounds represent 20 or 30 or 40 layers of covered-up garbage. Occasionally the mounds become unwieldy. Then it's time to level off the ground and start over.

In the past, this covering-up hasn't created much problem. Mankind consisted of separated pockets of civilization and the effect of waste on the world environment was minor, a local matter.

The attitude was, let's take care of our immediate problem and let the next generation take care of theirs. Even diseases have been comparatively limited in scope, mainly a local concern.

With all our progress in other ways, this attitude of the easy, immediate solution to waste is still with us in the industrial age. There has been no pause for a long-range look. Industry as yet has no real idea of the possible consequences of our vast collections of animal, chemical and mineral wastes.

Our cultural pattern has bogged down at the dumping stage. We still would rather dump into some nearby ravine or river. We still feel that when we can't see it, we don't have to worry about it.

For that reason, even when we start facing up to the pollution problem, we may have it out of proportion.

Dr. Tom Hogg, associate professor of anthropology at OSU, says most people think of pollution only in terms of air pollution, "because that's where you can see the pollution.

"Actually, there should be more concern about water pollution. You don't see water pollution, but it is probably more dangerous than air pollution."

Because we have never stopped to take stock, we have never developed the information we need to predict what pollution may do to us in the future. As a result, we have predictions on every side, wild, laughable, frightening.

"Until this century," said Dr. Davis, "We never have seen the need to take care of wastage. Up until now, man believed that normal dissolution and dissipation would take care of it."

But that no longer appears to be the case, because of that familiar ogre, rapid population growth. Now we are just beginning to see continent-wide influences of waste accumulation.

Population growth multiplies pollution. People increase arithmetically but technology expands geometrically.

"A person might produce a ton of waste a year but a machine can produce a ton of waste a day," Dr. Davis pointed out.

The facts of population growth are complicated further by the problem of our existing value system, particularly with respect to our economy.

We are taught to believe that the industrial system works profitably by producing goods as cheaply as possible. That means if you have a cheap means of waste disposal, you keep costs down.

Throughout man's history it has been held a great virtue to keep costs down. It was cheap labor that made the pyramids possible.

Dr. Davis, emphasizing that he was speaking as an observer of our scene rather than as an anthropologist, commented:

"You are practically flying in the face of God, country and mother if you suggest adding costs to production."

This feeling is evident most recently in the problem of field-burning in the Willamette Valley. The farmers claim they must burn in order to control insects and plant diseases.

However, it has come out that these farmers face an added cost of $12 an acre if they cannot burn, if they must dispose of the left-behind straw in some other way.

The insects and the diseases may well be rationalizations. Burning is the cheapest way to get rid of the waste.

Unfortunately, the cheapest possible way also provides the greatest amount of pollution possible, whatever the activity.

The automobile remains as one of our greatest pollutants, perhaps the greatest. Yet auto manufacturers continue to lag in the installation of anti-smog devices. Too expensive, they wail.

"I am consistently amazed at our attitudes toward long range planning," Dr. Davis said. "In this society, 10 years is a long range plan. Planning should be in hundreds of years, not 10s of years."

He continued: "We should take an Independent Blooper Machine (his term for an IBM computer), feed into it all the possible permutations of a waste product, and determine what can happen to it. Is it bio-degradable? Can it be made to be?"

In this belief, such a computer approach also should take into account all possible developments of new tools or technologies and learn all the offshoots that could result. The computer, with its high-speed ability to list all possible relationships, would provide a starting place for long range plans.

Dr. Davis gave an example of how short-range views may be creating long range disaster. Our government's AID program is devoted to soil development in foreign countries. The program uses defoliates for weed control and nitrates for better soil fertility.

Even now, scientists point out, nitrates are causing a pollution problem in this country. Nitrates are becoming concentrated in greater and greater amounts in the Mississippi River, the Gulf of Mexico and the Caribbean Sea.

Nitrate concentration fosters growth of oxygen-consuming organisms. These, in turn, reduce oxygen content of the water to the point where it will not support many species of sport and food fish.

However, the attitude of the AID field man is that the benefits of the soil program far outweigh any "minor" effects on the environment. And this is the story of our collective attitude on pollution. All you need are 20 or 30 different regions, each polluting in its own "minor way, and you can accumulate deadly doses.

Worst of all, you may be starting a process that is irreversible. It is believed that Lake Erie's degeneration from pollution is now irreversible. (*After aggressive counter-measures, Lake Erie is no longer considered dead.*)

The individual finds it hard to realize his own importance in this population-pollution spiral. He is still throwing his cigarette butts out the car window.

"Oh, come now," he says. "I don't toss out more than 10 butts a week. Does that make me a big, bad polluter?" Visualize

America's 30 million smokers each tossing out 10 butts a week from car windows for 52 weeks a year. Imagine how many tons of waste that will mean in one year.

Dr. Davis views the logger as one of our consistent examples of roadside pollution. You can follow the tracks of any logging operation by following the beer cans.

If man is by nature a polluter, it hasn't made so much difference up to now. But now we number humans in the billions. No other known mammal numbers even so much as one million. Quite possibly there are more humans than there are microbes of a given variety. We are everywhere, and we can no longer ignore our waste accumulation.

What are the solutions? The anthropologist urges long range planning, but something more is needed. We must change some fundamental attitudes.

For one, we have to admit that waste is a product of our life, just as much as the automobile or the TV set is a product of our life. We have to include waste in our life plan. Our goal is to get rid of that waste as best we can, which means the easiest and cheapest way with the least harmful consequences.

We have to admit that we do not have a value that fits this problem. There is no inner voice of conscience that says, "Thou shalt not dispose of thy waste in a manner that shall alter thine environment."

Dr. Davis, speaking again as a private citizen, declared, "We must put pressure on our industrialists and our government officials to bring waste disposal under the benevolence of God."

Difficult as such a change of values might be, it is possible. We did it with human and public sanitation. We believe that "cleanliness is next to Godliness" but it has only been in the last century that this has become a basic value.

Human sanitation began to be recognized with the development of biology and modern medicine. Before that, it was almost sinful to be too clean. W.H. Auden wrote a satiric line about not making love with those who wash too much. The hippie sub-culture rejected personal cleanliness as a sign of rejection of the entire dominant culture.

Florence Nightingale had to fight for hospital sanitation during the Civil War. Not until the late 19th century was it accepted that a surgeon should keep his instruments sterile.

Modern biology and medicine had discovered that personal and public sanitation was vital to disease control. From there, the campaign went to dissemination of information, to education of the public. As a result, there was a change of basic values.

If it could be done with human sanitation it can be done with environment sanitation. We already have frightening hints of the possible effects. But we do not yet have that drive to change our basic attitudes.

Change is being blocked by other conflicting values, such as the belief in the sanctity of the property owner and the right of business to be left alone, to operate as cheaply as it can.

However, let us not choose the corporation president and make him our scapegoat. He is tied to this value system as are you and I. He did not invent the rules, he just plays by them.

In the mystique of corporate business, he serves at the pleasure of the stockholders. He is an "employee," he protests, who has the responsibility to turn a profit. He can say, with truth, that if the annual dividend drops because he installs expensive anti-pollution equipment there will be screams at the annual meeting.

His protests are not entirely honest—he is often just ducking the responsibility. In every business there is some ultimate individual who can make the decision to control pollution and still not lose his job.

We should not forget, on the other hand, that many industrialists are taking leadership in pollution control. Anti-pollution devices are among the hottest manufacturing interests today. All of that acceptance cannot have come from outside pressure; there have to be some business leaders with a genuine sense of conscience.

At the government level, prospects for change may be brighter. It is now certain that in the 1970 elections we will have candidates campaign vigorously on anti-pollution platforms.

When we will elect politicians on their promises to clean up the environment and when we re-elect them according to how well they carry out these promises, we will know we are changing our basic values. We will know there is hope.

Unless it is already too late. Many people believe it is. As mentioned earlier, predictions have been wild, sometimes humorous, always grim.

One example: Engineers have been considering the pollution from an airplane exhaust at high elevations. The Boeing 707, traveling at 30,000 to 40,00 feet, will emit an exhaust which, it is said, will not precipitate out as a kind of ashy rain. It will simply hang there.

This accumulation of carbon dioxide and other gases will create a smog layer at high altitudes and an "energy trap" for solar radiation at ground level—a kind of world-wide temperature inversion.

As a result, the temperature of the earth will gradually rise significantly, enough to melt the polar ice caps and raise sea level as much as 250 feet.

First estimates indicated this should happen in about 200 years. A revised opinion holds that it will happen in 70 years.

If sea level rises 250 feet, 80 percent of the world's urban areas will be under water. Portland will become another Atlantis. Corvallis will be a seaport and Dr. Davis' home will be beachfront property.

Another OSU anthropologist, Dr. Carl Brown, has been delving into some recent speculations about population growth. There is now hope that we have enough technology to support gigantic population increases, although we will have to alter our life-style drastically.

As a side note, we cannot control population by exporting people to other planets. We would have to shoot off 60 million people every year to keep world population at our present level and they would quickly run out of planets to go to, or even moons of planets.

Even if our technology can feed and house all of us future masses, there still will be an upper limit beyond which population cannot go, according to this view.

This limit is set by the heat problem. As population becomes denser, heat increases. People and machines create heat. Using United Nations projections on population doubling, this theory states that unless population growth stops, within 890 years the earth will become too hot to support human life.

In the late stages of this super-hot culture, it would be a crime against society to cause needless heat.

"Voluntary exercise would not be permitted," said Dr. Brown. "You would have to give up jogging, it would create too much heat."

Dr. Brown, as do sober scientists generally, views these projections as possibility, not foreordained fact. Still, the warning is there. We must do something quickly or we create our own doom.

There is another possibility, that nature will take a hand in regulating our human approach to increasing pollution. As a result of natural selection, we may evolve a human who can breathe smog, eat garbage, drink sewage and still survive. In such a process, countless millions would not survive.

In the view of anthropology, our course against pollution is clear, even though difficult. We must reverse our human trait of being natural polluters.

We can do this through education. Through dissemination of information. Through pressure on industry to de-pollute, even if it means increased costs. Through election of officials who will treat pollution as the crisis it really is.

We will never do all this unless we change the basic value systems of our civilization.

We have to feel about waste the same way we feel about disease. We have to hate pollution even when we can't see it or smell it.

This has to be a gut feeling. We have to believe that a filthy world is just as evil as a filthy body.

11.16.69

"LET'S CLEAR THE AIR...":
THE FIGHT TO SAVE OUR HOME

Barry Lopez

L et's clear the air.
This planet you and I are standing on very graciously supports us. It gives us food, air, water, natural resources, and a place upon which to stand. But it is reaching the limit of its endurance. It has begun to cough and to show the first signs of pneumonia.

You know that. And you are probably tired of being told so. To save this planet, to seek a viable environment for mankind, has become our cause célèbre. It has become a social, a political, and an economic issue of the first magnitude. It has given us new words, like ecology and biodegradable and eutrophication. But it is also a movement that has waylaid us in the alley.

We have been run over, as if by a truck. We are intimidated and browbeaten by sudden, self-proclaimed experts, lectured to by bandwagon politicians, pacified by misleading advertising and left, in the end, confused: Confused about what it all means and what can be done.

There follows a list of books, a list of words, and a list of things that can be done. Hopefully they will clear the air of some of the confusion. Among the books you may find one or two that appeal to you. They are sane, logical and non-technical.

You've already seen most of the words, or will soon encounter them. At present they are horribly misused, even by the press. If you wish to do something, to set an example, to assuage your conscience, you may find the list helpful.

Books:

The Biological Time Bomb, Gordon Rattray Taylor. A popular best seller and a well-founded introduction to the phenomenal advances we've already made in the biological sciences. Taylor considers the impact of artificial inovulation, DNA manipulation, and the threat of chemical and genetic warfare, maintaining we are in dangerous control of processes we do not completely understand and are not capable of coping with, socially, politically or economically.

Silent Spring, Rachel Carson. A classic. An ethical scientist's reasoned attack on the irresponsible use of pesticides and insecticides.

Moment in the Sun, Robert and Leona Rienow. A forthright, frightening, and well-documented overview of our environmental problems.

The Frail Queen, Wesley Marx. A close and illuminating look at our often-ignored oceans, whose slow death could be the ultimate blunder.

The Quiet Crisis, Stewart L. Udall. An illustrated overview. The former Secretary of the Interior traces the historical relationships between Americans and the land, up to the present, no longer quiet, crisis.

Ecology, Peter Farb, et al. An excellent introduction to the notion of balance and purpose in nature.

The Population Bomb, Paul Ehrlich. An alarming look at the most basic problem—overpopulation. Ehrlich is blunt and practical in his analysis. A best-seller.

Voices for the Wilderness, edited by William Schwartz. A collection of sensitive, reasoned, and well-known essays taken from the Sierra Club Wilderness Conferences. Writers include Joseph

Wood Krutch, Stewart Udall, Ashley Montagu, William O. Douglas, and David Brower. Most of the essays have since appeared as articles. Paul Brooks' excellent "The Plot to Drown Alaska" appeared in the *Atlantic Monthly* and later in *Reader's Digest*.

The Web of Life, John H. Storer. One of the best of the overviews of ecology. Lucid, carefully written, and highly informative. His more recent *Man in the Web of Life* looks at modern man's political, social and economic problems as they relate to the future of his environment.

Science and Survival, Barry Commoner. A short, clear-cut, and excellent comment on the power, problems, and responsibilities of modern science.

Original Child Bomb, Thomas Merton. A very short, pointed history of the first atomic bomb. Subtitled *Points for meditation to be scratched on the walls of a cave.*

Also, *Audubon Magazine* and *Natural History*, which often carry excellent articles.

Words:

biodegradable: substances which can be broken down by bacterial action through decay. Substances which resist bacteria and represent inert, dead ends as steps in a food chain are non-biodegradable, like plastic.

biosphere: that part of the earth's surface and atmosphere where living organisms can exist.

ecology: the branch of biology which deals with organisms and their relationships to their environment. From ecos, home, and logos (to) study.

environment: all that impinges on the thing in question; the total surrounding, especially as it affects the growth or existence of that thing. From environ, meaning circle.

eutrophication: the process by which the oxygen content in water is reduced. An excess of nutrients, like phosphates and nitrogen compounds, spurs excessive algae growth. Such disproportionately large quantities of algae use more oxygen than they replace. Eutrophication polluted Lake Erie.

food chain: a series of organisms which pass on materials and energy by feeding on each other in a definite progression, usually larger eating smaller. Green plants, for example, are eaten by shrimp, which are then eaten by fish, which are then eaten by men. Food chains are highly complex and interrelated and intricately balanced. Man depends on them for his life.

nitrogen cycle: a continuous sequence of steps in which simple nitrogen compounds leave the soil-air-water, enter green plants, are broken down by bacteria, and return to the soil-air-water, to begin the cycle again. One of the most essential and basic of nature's cycles.

pesticide-insecticide: substances which are used to suppress or curb the populations of various organisms.

photosynthesis: the process by which all plant life, including our basic food-stuffs, grows, and by which water and carbon dioxide are changed into food and breathable oxygen.

pollution: a massive imbalance in an environment.

thermal pollution: results from a rise in the temperature of a natural body of water, even by as little as ½ a degree. Dams, which hold water still to "ake"under the sun in reservoirs, are a major cause of thermal pollution. Logging which removes shading trees at the edges of creeks and streams is another. Nuclear power plants are the newest threat. Thermal pollution grossly and adversely affects aquatic life by disrupting spawning activity and preventing annual migrations.

nitrate-phosphate pollution: caused primarily by fertilizer runoff and sewage disposal operations. Nitrate and phosphate compounds wash into streams and lakes and begin the process of eutrophication. The most uncontrolled and least recognized form of pollution.

particle pollution (a form of air pollution): caused primarily by carbon waste from automobile engines held in suspension in the atmosphere. Lead, which is highly poisonous, is another solid waste product of the auto engine.

sun: a source of light, heat, and energy whose rays, often cut off by air pollution, are critical to the maintenance of life; through the process of photosynthesis the sun functions as the source of all of man's energy, the first step in all food chains.

Things to do:
- Have no more than two children
- Buy milk in returnable bottles or containers
- Save newspapers and magazines and have them collected by agencies which will recycle them
- Use biodegradable soaps
- Avoid aerosol sprays: deodorants, hair sprays, table waxes, paint, etc.
- Don't burn trash, especially plastic
- Make use of car pools. If you can, walk or ride a bicycle
- Save aluminum cans: companies like Reynolds are paying ten cents a pound for them in Portland
- Use a reusable shopping bag for groceries
- Buy food in bulk containers with friends. Give what you don't want to charities, not to the dump
- Compost or bury garbage
- Start an organic garden (*How to Grow Vegetables and Fruits by the Organic Method*, by J.I. Rodale, et al; *Gardening With Nature* and *Make Friends With Your Land*, both by Leonard Wickenden)

The fight to save our home, this blue planet shimmering beneath a benevolent sun in the blackness of space, is a battle like none other we have ever fought. It is mankind's fight with himself. If he wins, he will have won himself. He could ask for no greater thing. If he loses, it will make no difference.

6.7.70

Portland's Air: Is It Doomed?
by Daniel Yost
8.13.72

"Our technological efforts are awesome almost beyond belief, but we have little energy left for basic work at home. Mary McCarthy, in a July 10 issue of *Newsweek*, said, 'In principle everybody is for the environment. In practice almost nobody is, chiefly because of general unwillingness to make the smallest immediate sacrifice in terms of comfort, speed or profit...'

"In the days ahead the City Council will debate an air quality plan. The issues will be out in the open along with the pollution. People of Portland will have an opportunity to decide what they regard as their well-being."

Do We Really Have A Right To A Clean Environment?
by Oral Bullard
4.10.77

"There is no longer a new land to which we can journey after we have fouled the old nest. In this way we have limited our freedom, and from that basis we must arrive at new decisions.

"What began, many years apart, as simple, good and basic urges—individual liberty and the preservation of the environment—have become complicated by their interaction one with another. The danger is that they will get bogged down in the arena of political, legal and bureaucratic opinion until we become convinced that they are somehow on a collision course—if one survives, the other must go. Somewhere along the line we will have to convert it to a win-win situation and prove we are big enough to accommodate both."

URSULA LE GUIN—IT'S TIME TO DECENTRALIZE

Daniel Yost

For Ursula Le Guin, Portland author of seven science fiction books (the latest of which is *The Lathe of Heaven*), the dilemma of individual freedom today is that the corporate and governmental super-agencies created out of the technology of the past 25 years are out of control and threatening the human beings who created them. In an interview at her home, she prefaced her remarks with a quote from Paul Goodman's book, *The New Reformation*.

"In all pre-revolutionary periods the regime becomes illegitimate, loses moral authority and has to rule by force. What's peculiar about our times is that because of the complexity of social, technical and urban organization, perhaps no central authority can be legitimate. It's bound to render the citizens powerless and to be dehumanizing. Then it is necessary to stop thinking in terms of power altogether."

From this point of departure, Ursula said:

"I think Goodman's right here. What's wrong with our new left and most of our attempts to do anything is that we're trying to work through the existing power structure or make a new one. But I don't think we can centralize anymore. We've got to change direction. Progress and growth are going to kill us within 20 or 30 years if we let corporations and government go on thinking that the only way to exist is to keep becoming bigger and heavier, more mechanized and consumerized. We've had it. We've got to start breaking up—decentralizing.

"In the 19th-century Socialism of William Morris, who was

an idealist and handicrafts man, we were supposed to go back and weave our own baskets and grow our own plants. He was foolish but in a sense he was right. I think today's crafts and good earth movements, particularly among the young, are right in the same way, but that's only part of it. We're not going to solve our problems just growing food on a few acres and trying not to be consumers. But this leads to politics, to a kind of participatory democracy which essentially means that in a city you start to work right where you are to make that part of the city better. You get local people and build from the bottom up instead of trying to rule everything from the top down."

But meanwhile, Ursula was asked, what do people do about national and international problems with time running out. Do we just sit and wait until we have worked up from the bottom?

"This is what scares me. I'm not sure we have the time. We're all scared. I think we all realize, even those who deny it, that we've done something awfully bad to the environment and it's getting worse all the time, and that overpopulation has to be checked. I think people are now willing to make sacrifices. We need a politician who will come along and call upon this groundswell of feeling the way McCarthy called upon our feelings about Vietnam. But look even at our Democratic candidates; not one of them has taken conservation or anything like that as a major issue. They never talk about it or say very little. Apparently they think they couldn't get elected that way. But the issues of population and the destruction of our environment are bigger than the war in a sense. I think they are crucial enough for people to respond to them.

"We should be able to solve our problems democratically in our genuine tradition. But most of us tend to think that the only way to handle something like the environmental crisis is by socializing a great many industries, by centralizing and getting more control, so we can slap down greedy businesses. And that may well be the only way if we keep going further and further with our environment wrecking goods and materials. But if it is, we are going to have an absolutely repressive time of it. It will extend to individuals in that government may have to say, sorry, no more dishwashers, baby, because we can't have detergents anymore. Government may have to stop the manufacture of plastics, which already will be polluting us for the next 10,000 years because they're indestructible."

What kind of a curtailment of freedom do we have today from government, she was asked?

"Today, of course, we have government encouraging business growth, encouraging the large corporation that either makes money or war as against the individual consumer or soldier. The individual is treated only as a member of an enormous mass. I think this is essentially anti-democratic and disastrous, leading to a future of repressive controls."

Are the people aware of the possibility of this future curtailment of freedom?

"No, I don't think so. None of our leaders are talking about it. But maybe they don't really believe it yet. They keep thinking, oh well, a few more plastic bags won't hurt.

"But our people know there's a crisis and I think they would help, like the English did under the austerity program during and after World War II, like people did here to a lesser degree, if someone would point out the challenge. We can stop, we can cut down. It might even come as a relief. Any religious person would say, of course, that true freedom is gained by giving up things, possessions. And that's a very strong streak in human nature. We all know we're imprisoned by things, money, by buying and selling. And I think when we realize what the priorities really are, that our children's survival is at stake and maybe our own, we would be happy to do something instead of sitting and watching things get worse and the smog get thicker."

2.13.72

MIKE RUSSO—IT DOESN'T
LOOK VERY HOPEFUL

Daniel Yost

In an interview at his studio, Mike Russo, highly regarded Portland artist, began with an expression of pessimism about the direction our country is headed in the area of individual freedom and tied problems in this area at home with attitudes that are translated into policy abroad.

How does this affect civil liberties?

"Forces which are in command and perpetuate the war are the same forces that stifle the movement of civil liberties in this country. What seemed at one time to be a very promising upsurge for peace and civil liberties has been largely checkmated."

Are blacks and other minority groups making progress today, or is this illusionary?

"I don't see it as real progress. I think this is true of the whole history of the question. Ever since the Civil War it could be said that the blacks have been making progress. Some people go so far as to say that they have it better in this country than anywhere else. But in relation to the problem as it exists today, I think that the situation is worse than it ever has been. The problem daily grows more acute, the moral crisis becomes greater, and we are not keeping pace with it. So I would say we are losing ground."

How would you define the gains blacks are making?

"At this point I would say it doesn't look very hopeful. The inability to put a stop to the Vietnam war has produced an enormous moral defeat, not only for the American people, but also for the entire civil rights movement. The winding down of the war is a kind of false promise. Actually we are carrying on the war in the manner it was started, to its ultimate conclusion which suits our purposes. I think we will continue to maintain forces in Asia like we do in Europe and this will be simply another episode in the kind of foreign policy that so many today object to and regard as immoral.

"Sometimes the gains that are made are only another method for perpetuating inequalities. They alleviate certain symptoms in a way which makes possible an indefinite continuation of the inequalities. Certain tantalizing promises are made to blacks to attain some of the middle class aspirations. The idea of giving them a hunk of the economy, a share in the prosperity, is sort of a bribe."

This is not related to gaining freedom?

"No, this is a way of tempting participation in the enterprise system but it does not reach down and produce the kind of equality that the total black population needs. Some of the banking ideas, the attempts to finance banking enterprises under the sponsorship of blacks; this is telling blacks they are achieving equality and also telling whites that they are doing something. But I think the real problem is, for example, in unemployment. There is a great disproportionate relationship between blacks and whites here."

Do you think the white North really wants integration?

"The North has shown an equal or perhaps greater resistance to integration than the South. Because we have fewer blacks in some parts of the North, many people feel that we don't have as much of a problem. But this is not the case at all."

How does the moral crisis you mentioned affect the civil liberties of the ordinary citizen, white as well as black?

"Actually the administration is attempting to create a lull, trying to appeal to certain sensibilities. This is a strategy to checkmate all reform. The country is tremendously in need of all kinds of reform and there is a great deal of sentiment for reform. But the Nixon administration has no intention of serving this purpose and is doing everything possible to play down these needs. For example, I think law and order as a slogan is an attempt to switch the attention of the people from needs to what the administration prefers. I think Attica is an example of the need for reform on the one hand and the use of law and order to suppress reform and conceal the real issues on the other."

In your view, what are these real issues?

"That the prison system is outmoded and inhuman. That places like Attica are more like race compounds than prisons. The conditions have long called for reform, but the establishment has not moved to bring it about, instead retaliating with this idea of law and order. The suppression of civil rights and the rigid methods that are being used have a tendency to create a very explosive situation. The quiet and tranquility is deceptive because underneath is a smoldering fire capable of blazing into more and more episodes like Attica."

What is your opinion of the growing files of information stored at credit bureaus? Are we moving towards full-scale government snooping and such things as a central data bank?

"This again is a kind of tradition in our society. More and more the argument is being made that this is the normal requirement of everyday life, that the country can't be managed with any efficiency unless this information is on hand, that our security depends on it. I think this also grows out of war conditions."

Do you think certain authorities have a preconception about what kind of human being is needed in order for them to run their idea of government with maximum efficiency?

"I would say the authorities don't have any faith in human beings and therefore really don't believe in human rights. Everybody is potentially a dangerous person and so must be watched. They anticipate criminal behavior from everyone so they want a line on everyone. This is really not the purpose of a decent society which has regard for human values."

How can we reverse this kind of government?

"I'm very pessimistic about politics. Frankly I see no solution in the two-party system. Just as LBJ was no alternative to Goldwater, so Nixon was no alternative to LBJ and I'm not sure the next administration will be an alternative to the present situation. I think what we need in our country is a very powerful independent force which, if it didn't win the election, at least could exercise an enormous influence and pressure for change."

2.13.72

LET'S NOT OVERREACT

Larry Leonard

If bombings bother you, you're normal. If they make you mad, you are part of the establishment—on a purely statistical basis, at least. It is the one part of the revolution that the average guy fully understands—and would like to fight. The question, obviously, is how?

So, I park across from the headquarters of the establishment and walk to the only door that is open, the Broadway entrance. It is the only open door because that way you can keep an eye on folks coming into the building and maybe spot an incoming bomber.

One door! It's like the Old West when they closed the doors of the fort in preparation for Indian trouble. Only one way to get in and talk to people, you know.

The people in the elevator eye me carefully because I have a beard and all terrorists have beards. At the fourth floor, I find a door that says FBI. I am standing and looking at the Most Wanted photos on the wall and realize that about a third of these legendary criminals are young and non-criminal types. They are youthful, middle-class women who look like they could whip up a cookie for a hungry boy. Yet here they are with the armed robbers and other felons.

The door to a side office opens and Julius Mattson, special agent in charge of the Portland office, ushers someone out.

"Hey," I tell him, "this guy looks just like me."

"That," he replies, "illustrates part of the problem we are going to talk about."

I talked with Mattson—more on that later—and I talked with U.S. District Judge Alfred T. Goodwin. Surprisingly, the answer to that question, how to fight the bombers, was not the suggested formation of units of glossy-domed leather men with oak hands to batter the furies into submission. Far from it, in fact. They hold that any revolutionary who resorts to bombing or destruction of property is a criminal and should be treated accordingly. But extreme care must be taken to see that in these dealings we don't deprive others of their freedoms of speech and assembly.

The establishment, they believe, could destroy America more effectively than any revolutionary movement if to put down dissention those guarantees were abrogated.

"This is the big danger," says another establishment defender, U.S. Attorney Sid Lezak. "We must not overreact or we will create the fascist state the revolutionaries say already exists. Suppression of dissent is not the answer."

Just how the establishment will attempt to walk this scary thin line between justice and over-reaction is the question we will seek to answer here. But, first, a surprising opinion held by the men we interviewed—a viewpoint that sets up some interesting questions of its own.

Now, to the interviews. Mattson's office is almost Spartan; just a large desk, a flag and a large photograph of J. Edgar Hoover. Mattson is my idea of a special agent for the FBI. He is of medium height, ruggedly good-looking with a strong broad nose, an important jaw and cool blue eyes. He smokes Camels.

"Terrorism," says Mattson, "is priority with us. You saw that on our Most Wanted board outside. Our problem with terrorists here as in other areas of the country is public support for the offender. That's why this type of criminal is so difficult to apprehend. He melts right into the vast protesting mass and they cover him completely.

"Who are the terrorists? That's hard to say. They are young, generally, and often aligned with a political faction of militant views like the Black Panthers, the SDS or the Minutemen. Far right or far left, it creates the same problem for us. Violence is bad no matter who's at fault, including the FBI."

Define that violence. What are the weapons? "Terrorists prefer incendiary explosives, and the new laws focus on them."

If the terrorists are young, and if their weapons are explosives, where and how do they learn to use these devices? "In most instances, they pick the information from the pages of pamphlets or publications of militant groups. I've seen instruction books put out by the SDS and the Panthers that give detailed descriptions of the types of bombs we've encountered. This is dangerous. You need to know a lot more than you can learn from an article if you hope to build an effective time explosive. These things often blow up in the faces of the builders."

These builders are, you have said, often aligned with militant organizations. It has been said that, because of this, the FBI maintains infiltrators in the colleges and universities. Paid spies.

"We've received flak from Salem about this in recent weeks. It's not true. First, the paid informer concept implies we take the offensive in this thing. We don't. There are individuals in the universities who agree with the goals of many of the movements—as many of us within the FBI do—but simply cannot condone violence as a method of achieving those goals. These people frequently offer their assistance and we gladly accept it."

Are they paid? "For out-of-pocket expenses, yes. For wages lost if they take time off from work, yes. As for a salary or a formal employee relationship, that is simply not true. The only people on salary here are the regular agents."

Speaking of the agents, Mr. Mattson, how will their work be affected by the new bill Mr. Nixon signed into law?

"More help, of course, since some of the 1,000 new agents will be coming here. But, more important, the new areas of coverage broaden and clarify our responsibilities."

Elaborate on that. "Well, attempts to transport explosives with intent to violate federal statutes. And the willful making of a false threat by instrument of commerce—the telephone or the mail, for example, to perform the same. Possession without written permission within any federal building or the use of explosives against equipment used in interstate commerce or even equipment that supports that equipment is now illegal on the federal level. And most important, the scope of federal responsibility has been broadened to include any institution receiving federal funds."

A school for example. "Exactly."

So you and your men will now investigate terrorist activities like the bombs that went off on the University of Oregon campus. "As long as the school receives federal funding of any kind and an FBI investigation is authorized by the Justice Department."

I gather from all this, Mr. Mattson, that you don't—I mean the FBI doesn't concern itself with anything before the fact. "You mean the causes? That's true on an official level, but each man here is a taxpayer and an average citizen just like you. On a personal level, especially since we're so close to the trouble, many of us do as much as we can to solve some of the problems."

Working against poverty and racism and the like?

"That, of course. But there's more. Voting for and supporting in other ways the legislators and programs we believe will go far toward helping. Policemen, for example. There aren't enough in this country. In the past, 2.2 for every 1000 of population was fine; but with the rising crime rate, plus the new politically oriented terrorism, we need more. More of them, well qualified and adequately trained.

"And our laws need updating—to correct inequities in the old ones, and protect against new types of crime with new ones. And, the courts. They're overloaded so badly that there have been instances where it's taken eight years to dispose of a case. Eight years! And speaking of overcrowding, while Oregon institutions are doing pretty good in general, our penal system nationally isn't. They're understaffed, underfinanced, out of date and provide inadequate opportunity for rehabilitation. It's a bad situation, and only money can get things moving. We support those measures whenever possible.

"I think the general public should be more alert to necessary financial and social remedies to improve our system of criminal justice."

Noon on the following day. I went into the private chambers of Federal Judge Alfred T. Goodwin. In case you've never seen a judge's chambers, this one is perhaps fifteen by eighteen feet, contains the same simple government furnishings that

Mattson has with the addition of floor-to-ceiling walls full of hardbound law books. High on one wall hung a framed poster of almost pop-art design featuring the following inscription: "I should like to be able to love my country and still love justice— Camus."

Judge Goodwin walks in, removes his robe and shakes hands. He is of the same broad-featured school as Mattson, though larger in frame and a bit more forceful in proclamation.

We tell him we have noted a concern over public apathy toward the activities of terrorists and ask if he feels it, too. If so, what might be its cause?

"It is there," said Goodwin, "and I believe it's due to overexposure—and I don't want to have this turn out as a condemnation of the media—to too much violence. You read about it everyday, and you see it on TV. Think it's almost to the point with some people where you get more ink out of shooting a cougar than this other."

Who, Judge Goodwin, are the terrorists?

"Alienated people. Disassociated and alienated. I think a lot of them have distorted martyr complexes. Samson complexes. They want to pull down the temple, you know."

Why do they want to do this? "There is some rational background to the current dissension, of course. Hypocrisy is one cause. The kids see it and don't like it. Like the laws against juveniles smoking cigarettes, but machines everywhere so anyone with the money can break the law. And the moral laws are often selectively enforced. Adultery is obviously quite common. Too, the kids see their parents get smashed at a party and then risk peoples' lives on the road. Then these same parents become hysterical at the very mention of marijuana, which the kids claim offers far better individual control than alcohol without the other possible effects aside."

Seems to be a thread here. The kids don't like moral laws. "As I see it, their feeling is that society should not punish crimes without victims."

How about the war? Has Vietnam spurred terrorism? "Obviously it has. The bombings of recruiting offices could represent nothing else. Five or six years ago, the kids were adamantly opposed to this war, an opening wedge for alienation. Things have obviously changed there."

Unpopular ideas can become popular ones. "Exactly. And I don't think the terrorists helped things at all. It was the peaceful resisters who conscientiously disagreed in non-violent forms, and paid the penalty that society imposed—prison for refusing induction."

Improved communications could help? "I get a new law clerk every year—have been for the past 11 years. They're here to learn from us, but I'm amazed at how much I can learn from them. They're getting smarter and smarter. They've been shelled with tear gas, hassled by the police. They've written for the underground presses and now they're integrating into society and changing it as they go."

You believe, then, that change is needed? "Certainly, and it is dramatic how much of that change is coming through the courts. And, how much more could if more people would use the tools available by law."

Explain. "Well, I remember a case some years back. A company with a dirty smokestack dumping soot on private homes. Finally, someone got a lawyer, of all things, and took the firm to court. A private individual against a mighty corporation. And, of course, he won and the company had to put a cap on their stack or pay continuing damages to half a town.

"And I presided over a case of an unmarried woman from Sweden who applied for naturalization. It turned out that she was living with a man, so an immigration official interpreted the morality segment of the statutes to be against allowing her request. Finally, it came to my court and I ruled that she should be allowed her opinion that as far as she could see, American style marriage was unsuccessful, and she preferred to live by her own personal standards. The case is on appeal."

So, you maintain that some of the moral, social and ecological changes that need to be made can be best accomplished through the courts. "Exactly."

So, that is where these men in the establishment stand. They have carefully chosen their words for these interviews, but in their favor is the fact that much rhetoric has gone before and people are on edge. And, their big boss says it is now time to defuse the violence.

They do not like the bomber, regardless of his motives. Build, baby, build! They believe the courts can contribute dramatically as soon as the average citizen understands where and how he can obtain free legal service.

12.13.70

The ACLU: Reexamining Our Rights
by Oral Bullard
7.4.76

"The ACLU has been damned by the right, the left and the middle. It has defended Communists, Nazis, kids with long hair and, in a celebrated Oregon case that went to the U.S. Supreme Court, a Vietnam protester who was barred from passing out anti-war leaflets in the Lloyd Center. It has defended unpopular issues and individuals whose causes it did not espouse for the simple reason it believed those individuals' Constitutional rights were being violated.

"...Civil liberties have always been won by dissent, the American Revolution being a prime example. But the search for freedom began long before that, and somewhere, in some unrecorded time, some person rose to defend himself against the transgressions of the governing group—and in that moment the first civil libertarian was born."

The Changing Family

IS THE FAMILY BECOMING EXTINCT?

Art Chenoweth

If there is one aspect of American society everyone agrees on, it is the "breakdown" of the family. No matter the statistics used, the signs of "decay" are obvious: more divorce, not quite enough remarriage, too much single parenting, increased sexual "permissiveness" or experimentation.

Many people (not all) relate these symptoms to other social ills: growing violence and crime, especially juvenile crime, abortion, widespread venereal disease, drug abuse, child abuse and sexual harassment, to name a few.

All this apparent decay has proved an affront to the White Anglo-Saxon Protestant work ethic, actually shared in this country by Catholics and even Hindus. Most, maybe all, the defects of society have been traced to this breakdown of the nuclear family—a kinship group consisting only of parents and unmarried offspring.

Others go back further and say that the beginning of the trouble was the breakdown of the extended family—the kinship group consisting of other relatives, in addition to parents and unmarried offspring.

The WASP reaction to this sense of decay has been to fight it, saying, "We've got to get back to the good old-fashioned virtues." Some of this reaction has been positive, producing programs to improve relationships among family members. Some reaction has been violently negative, such as the resurgence of the Ku Klux Klan, the neo-Nazis and "gay-bashing" attacks on homosexuals. Some has been less violently negative, trying to bring back the respect for (or fear of) parental or paternal authority, the devotion to uncomplaining hard work, the deference to one's "betters" and the willingness to be bottom dog for a while in hope that one someday may be top dog. Whether such virtues ever actually existed, except in the minds of some of the top dogs, is debatable. In the drive to restore this vanished and probably mythical state of family harmony, campaigns have been organized to teach creationism; to forbid abortion; to crack down on homosexuals, especially lesbian mothers; to restrict access to contraception.

Any study of the development and evolution of the family based on actual field data would lead to the conclusion that, while positive efforts may ease the strains, neither they nor the negative influences are likely to have much, probably not any, long-range effect on the continued and inevitable evolution of the family.

A second, and happier, conclusion would be that the family is here to stay, however strained its present condition may seem. This is not the Day of Doom. More likely it is a period of painful transition—rather rapid transition, much too rapid for many.

A third possible conclusion is that the nuclear family itself is not all that great; in fact it could be seen as about the worst possible family grouping, when considered in the entire range of past and present family structures. So maybe its breakdown is just as well.

With the nuclear family, the institution of family has shrunk about as far as it can, and almost any other movement is up. However, even though the nuclear family may be "worst," its development was almost inevitable in the context of the industrialization of America.

So it isn't anybody's fault that the American family finds itself in such disarray. This situation has come from an almost inexorable march of circumstances, although influenced significantly by the culture. The march is inexorable, and where it is to lead probably also is inexorable.

It is to be recognized that no matter what point of view this article takes, it is certain to be criticized by all manner of experts, from sociologists to creationists. There is no unanimity. This is a point of view and, in the words of a charming old book on bartending, "under no circumstances can correspondence on the matter be entertained."

Life is said to be too short, but in other ways it is too long. We live so short a time that we think of current society as "the way it is" and fail to see that it hasn't always been that way, maybe not even for very long. Along with that goes the romanticizing of the good old days, an indication that we live too long. Change occurs, but not enough in a lifetime for us to see the major outlines.

As a defining point, this article will consider the family evolution primarily from a "state of the art" position in anthropology called sociobiology, presented by Pierre L. van den Berghe in his lengthy study, *Human Family Systems: An Evolutionary View.* Daniel Scheans, professor of anthropology at Portland State University, has added comments and illuminations. Neither van den Berghe nor Scheans claims this is the only possible point of view; they admit it may clash with views held by others. However, it is a view substantiated by the best available hard evidence from studies of many families in many societies the world over.

Unfortunately, unlike in zoology, there are no fossilized families that may be dug up and studied. Fortunately, there are today still some examples of all types of family structure along the evolutionary trail, although some of the most rudimentary of them are shrinking fast as the world shrinks.

Sociobiology is defined as the application of Darwinian evolutionary theory to animal behavior—"animal" including man. Right there, you lose the creationists, but sociobiology here is not comparing creationism with the Big Bang Theory. In fact, creationists would be interested to know that the Bible illustrates sociobiology perfectly. King Solomon's many wives contrasted with monogamy today; Jacob's 14 years of servitude to acquire two wives, two serving maids and a flock of livestock fit perfectly into the theories of sociobiology.

Briefly, in this point of view, nature rules. There is an ingrained need, an obsession, to reproduce and have the children nurtured to maturity so they can in turn reproduce. This need impels humans to form pairs, or pair-bonds, which usually means marriage, leading to child-bearing. This is more than some vague drive "to perpetuate the species." It is a specific drive to perpetuate one's own individual combination of genes. Human mating patterns and family structures are seen as basically designed to that end, while making necessary adaptations to the environment.

This position places sociobiology in some opposition to "cultural determinism," which implies less influence from biology and more from environment. On the other hand, it is not the rigid biological determinism that argues that all characteristics are genetically determined. Van den Berghe says:

"People like Arthur Jensen, who make silly statements such as that 80 percent of the variance in intelligence is inherited, are not competent geneticists; they are biologically naïve psychologists."

Van den Berghe amplifies his point of view this way:

"Natural selection theory is not a theory of rigid genetic determination, as social scientists sometimes misrepresent it to be. It is a theory of the interplay of genotype (the genetic makeup of an organism) and environment, an environment which, for humans, includes culture...Culture is a way our species has of adapting fast to changes in the environment, including those changes that have been induced by the culture itself. But culture does not happen in a biological vacuum...Humans are quite adaptable, but not randomly or infinitely so...All human societies are organized, at least partially, on the basis of mating and reproduction."

Van den Berghe emphasizes that "Culture...grew out of nature, not to overrule it, but to add on to it."

This is not to imply that the human is just a higher type of animal, for the human has something no other being has, consciousness of its own behavior. Only the human is conscious of its own behavior, able to worry, dream, scheme, plan, invent, analyze, and experience its experience, savor it, act on it. Only humans find sex to be such fun.

If all of family and society is the drive to reproduce individual genes, where does that leave romantic love? Sociobiology has a place for that.

"Mates stick together, not so much because they 'love' each other but for the fitness of the young, which is also the fitness of their own genes. At the root of both parental and conjugal love is, once again, the ultimate genetic egoism. Mates 'fall in love' or, more prosaically, become imprinted on each other, in species where it serves their individual fitness to do so. Sexual love, in the last analysis, is genetic self-love."

So, back to square one of this story of family forming and family evolving, keeping in mind this is a vast oversimplification. The detailed source material is easily available.

We find a human being driven, obsessed, with the need to reproduce not merely its own species but the specific gene pattern carried within the individual.

This drive to mate and reproduce leads to marriage. The minimum definition of marriage given by Scheans is two people living together in a socially recognized way. Van den Berghe's definition is socially sanctioned mating in humans. It need have nothing to do with ceremonies.

A pair-bond is a stable mating relationship between an individual male and a female.

Mating, marriage, pair-bonding leads to family organization, which depends on many factors—the environment, the culture, the most efficient, the most effective, the most "fit" way to mate, reproduce and pass along those genes.

In this the woman has some disadvantage and some advantage, as does the man. The woman can produce a limited number of children. She is not a frog, potentially reproducing millions. On the other hand, she has one great advantage. When she has a child, she knows it is hers, unless a switch was made at the hospital.

The man has no such assurance. The old saw is true: "It is a wise child that knows its own father." The man who sires sons has a statistically better chance of passing along his genes than a woman who bears daughters, but the big rub is, has the man actually fathered that son? Men are not that reproductively efficient. The biologically safe solution is for the man to mate early and often and with many. That way, he has the best chance of passing along the genes. Of course, some of these offspring must survive.

As a result of these inequalities, women are the ultimate scarce resource for men. If a man wants to reproduce his genes, the safest way is to have as many women as possible. Males therefore compete for females. Females are choosier than males, because their reproductive mistakes are costlier than those of males.

Once the "inner" man realizes this, his craving for women deepens. Women become society's most sought-after commodity. This explains why polygyny, the stable mating between a man and two or more females, is socially acceptable in the vast majority of human societies.

And who always accumulates the most of the scarcest commodity? The rich, of course. So the rich acquire the multiples of women. Since there are naturally only about enough women to go around, one to each man, this means there are going to be a lot of bachelors who never have any women at all, and even most of the polygynous men have no more than two wives. So, although polygyny is socially acceptable in most societies, it is, in practice, much rarer than monogamy.

Also, in most societies there is a limit to how many babies can be brought into the world and still survive to maturity. So, many societies have some form of population control, even the polygynous ones, from contraception to the killing of excess babies.

Until the spread of Christianity, societies enforcing monogamy by law were "exotic exceptions." As Scheans put it, Solomon with all his wives and concubines "didn't know why he did it, but he felt better doing it."

This alleged scarcity of women may seem a puzzle to many women complaining about the "shortage of men." Without attacking that problem in detail, we may suggest that these women are merely exercising their biological need to be "choosier than males."

Van den Berghe summarizes this mechanism as follows:

"…One of the first forms of investment of wealth, as soon as surplus could be created through agriculture and animal domestication, has been matrimonial. Men and their male kinsmen in patrilineal descent (line of descent through the males) have invested in women to secure access to and control of the reproductive power of as many of them as possible."

In modern American society, a man is allowed but one wife. But isn't that still one of the envied prerogatives of the rich American man, his ability to accumulate quantities of women, even though they can't be legally sanctioned? The Mormons practiced polygyny, a sensible choice in view of their situation, and some still may practice it quietly. The Mormon experiment faltered, said Scheans, because these people were of European background with notions about romantic love. Inevitably, jealousies broke out. Under a better-evolved system, the first wife should have become "lead wife," a kind of executive wife over the other wives.

So, in the evolution of the family, the two most common forms have been one man-one woman and one man-multiple women. Other forms have not worked out, and have not provided human satisfaction. Group marriages and forms of polyandry—one woman-multiple husbands—are rare and not expected to increase. Promiscuity, homosexuality, abstinence and celibacy also don't pan out for the majority in the long run. There is no documented case of a matriarchy, where a woman runs the show. Alas for the feminists, men have always ruled, no matter what the family form and no matter whether the descent is patrilineal (through the males), matrilineal (through the females) or bilateral (giving equal significance to all ancestors).

No human society known to science has ever institutionalized promiscuity, group marriage or "swinging" as the most common form of mating. Many, however, permit "interludes," of which the most American is the office Christmas party.

Other factors are at work in family formation and evolution, such as fitness (a measure of reproductive success), kin selection (we call it nepotism), reciprocity (doing unto others so they will do likewise unto you) and coercion (the use of threat or force to modify the other person's behavior).

Monogamy is the most frequent arrangement, but the vast majority of societies allow polygyny—or did until they were conquered by monogamous societies. All cultures have some division of labor by sex, both in society and the family. Women tend to do the at-home production, men the long-distance work. Practically all have taboos against incest. Most mated couples share a home that is defended territory. They may not live alone, however, but in a shared compound or group dwelling.

The studies of families show just a few general types, relating considerably to the type of economy. Strangely, the most advanced, our present industrial family, resembles most the simplest, the hunting and gathering family.

The first and simplest type of family is the highly flexible, stateless (i.e. no formation of a political state) family of hunters, fishermen and gatherers. Next step is the highly structured but still stateless horticultural-pastoral society. These people are gardeners; they slash and burn, they do not plow. The next evolution is into the agrarian society, the society of the peasant. From there it is the industrial society, extremely flexible but a lot of state.

The hunting and gathering society likes mobility and will move about even when it has enough to eat and drink in its present location. There are small local kin groups which people move into and out of easily. Line of descent is bilateral, all ancestors equally important, or patrilineal, through the males. There is no state. The family is nuclear, husband, wife, few children. Inheritance amounts to little; there is little to inherit. A few men may have more than one wife. There are few marriage rules, except for incest.

Partners often choose each other from the available candidates, often with some advice from relatives. There is a form of courtship, gift exchange between families, sometimes "bride service," which means the husband works for his father-in-law for a stated period of years.

The next stage, stateless horticulturalists, has much more structure. The system of production is more efficient; therefore populations are denser and societies larger. Competition creates more of a need for kinship strength. Surplus production makes some richer than others, and the surplus is invested in reproductive women, scarcest resource of all for men.

In this society, some may claim to be or would like to be chief. Classes are being formed. There is slavery. The new importance of kinship introduces the extended family. There is less choice of residence; it is usually with the groom's father's family, less often the bride's father's family. The rule of descent usually goes through the male line, sometimes the female. Frequently there are quite rigid rules about who is eligible to marry whom. Marriages are arranged; the partners have very little to say about it. The groom or groom's family generally must pungle up some material goods to secure the bride. This is not so much "buying a bride" as compensating the bride's family for the loss of the most valuable and scarce commodity, a reproductive woman.

In the next stage, the agrarian society, the state becomes established. The family or kinship group, clan, tribe, begins to lose its political functions to the state. Polygyny still exists, but it is more and more restricted to the people who can afford it, the ruling classes, who use their wealth to buy more women or, biologically speaking, to improve their reproductive fitness.

This agrarian society is extremely bureaucratized and has elaborate and rigid class systems including slavery. The family may be extended or perhaps "stem," a kin group consisting of parents, their unmarried offspring and one married son with his wife and children. This may be accompanied by primogeniture, inheritance by the oldest child, frequently the oldest male child. Young couples live with the groom's parents, typically, in this society and descent may be through the males only or all descendants. The peasants, of course, cannot afford more than one wife, so they settle for monogamy if they are able to secure even one wife. There are many rules about who can marry whom. Marriages are arranged by families from a fairly large field of candidates, and the partners do have some say about it.

There is likely to be gift exchange between families. There may even be a dowry, property that goes along with the bride. However, this is the bride's property, not the groom's. This is what gave Henry II of England fits. He wanted his wife, Eleanor of Aquitaine, to sign over her dower property—she owned what amounted to a couple of provinces. Wisely, she didn't want to give them away; they were her life insurance. Small wonder at her reluctance, considering the shabby way Henry treated her. But then, that seems to have been the fate of women since the family began. Men, always driven to fertilize yet another female, will always desert them if they can get away with it, provided there is some likelihood of the existing offspring surviving. Also, in many societies, women are beaten regularly by their husbands, often kidnapped, routinely raped, sometimes even eaten, forced to do the most menial tasks and after all that, required to do the job of child-rearing, which most men find unbearable.

As van den Berghe says, "Even in highly affluent societies, there is still no good, efficient, cheap substitute for mothers."

If the woman is put upon in all societies, imagine the lot of the woman in agrarian society, particularly the peasant woman.

As Scheans pointed out, the peasant suffers from the problem that he can never quite get even with the game because he has three demands on his resources, and one of them will always get him.

First is his replacement demand, which is what he has to do to feed himself, keep a supply of tools, keep up any personal livestock he may need. Then there are the strident social-religious demands that he cannot, seemingly, avoid. Remember, agrarian society is not a simple society. His social demands include his extended family. True, it has advantages. It can function as his welfare source, his bank, his source of comfort, medical services, legal advice, help in a fight. But the extended family also makes its demands. The demands you put on your relatives your relatives can put on you. Your relatives can bleed you dry.

There also are demanding religious obligations. For example, the peasants of Southern Italy invest in elaborate religious ceremonials centering on the Madonna rather than on Jesus.

The third demand on the peasant is his rent, what he must

pay to the land-owner to continue to occupy the land and derive his sustenance.

The agrarian society has evolved into the most complex society of all, the industrial. That's where we find ourselves in America today, or maybe a little past, in some kind of post-industrial society.

By now, as we all know from experience, the family has lost to the state all its political functions, most of its economic functions and almost all of its educational functions. The state controls all. Industrial production means that the land no longer is the support of the citizen; it is the sweat of his brow, his labor.

When labor becomes the basis of individual sustenance, the worker must be kept mobile, which means the family must be kept small. The family is reduced to its simplest form, turning full circle and, to some degree, back to where the hunters and gatherers found it. It is the monogamous nuclear family: husband, wife, unmarried children. It is semi-nomadic. It is neolocal, meaning we don't live with the folks any more, we start "a home of our own." That can be depressing, for now it is "us against the world." As in the simple society, there are few, if any, rules concerning marriage, except incest, although we tend to marry "within our class." Descent is recognized through both sides of the family, male and female.

In what could be interpreted as a gloomy outlook, van den Berghe suggests that here we find "an irreducible minimum of human mating and reproductive systems without which we would not be fully human." At least, attempts to eliminate the family, even in that minimum form, have so far proven both unsatisfying and unworkable.

Contraception is widespread, the number of children born growing smaller. With such fierce competition in the economic and class world, "better to have only two children who are university graduates with good jobs; a secure income and a good home…than eight badly educated, underfed children who are likely to become juvenile delinquents, to be shot by the police or locked up under conditions of compulsory celibacy…so that…they may end up producing few or no grandchildren."

Another factor may be decreasing the number of children, the feeling that you can't raise a bunch of kids and still enjoy the "good life" of technology, travel and titillation. Even the rich, who could afford it, apparently would rather be free to be artists or jet-setters than stay home and raise rug rats.

In industrial society, the poor, particularly the urban poor, appear to play a peculiar role, somewhat like that of the simple hunter and gatherer who must locate near the source of economic supply.

This the urban poor do. They have that same inner drive to reproduce their genes, and they can have a lot of children because they are thereby improving their biological fitness without risking much else.

The source of supply to the urban poor is now the state. They can have children or, if they choose, give up some to state-paid abortion. They can live on welfare and food stamps, cashing in the food stamps (quite easy to do) to buy six-packs of beer, cigarettes, plays at the pin-ball machine and other adequate sources of recreation. Under food stamps, they are permitted to buy candy, pop, potato chips and even bubble gum. If they are veterans, the state will even bury them and throw in a beautiful U.S. flag.

The industrial family, urban poor or affluent jet-setter, is designed, just as all the family types are designed, to "make the best of available resources given the level of technology, or, in other words, to maximize individual benefits."

This overview omitted some important characteristics of the American family that are all too familiar to most of us. To say that there are no extended families is not completely true; yet having aged parents in the house is always thought of as temporary. Far better, if necessary, to have a separate "mother-in-law apartment" because "Mother would rather have it that way."

The nuclear, mobile family is neither "good" nor "bad"; it is. It remains the norm because no satisfactory substitute has been found for rearing children in the present society, especially children up through five or six years.

The Japanese industrial family is not completely comparable.

Centuries of culture still weigh on Japanese preferences and have been adapted to the industrial society. The corporation has tended to become the kinship, complete with ceremonials and other paternalistic gimmicks. That system has been transplanted to at least one factory in America run by Japanese, and the results have seemed to be quite good, although the Americans balked at scheduled exercise classes.

All this still leaves us with the crisis in the American family. By reducing itself to the simplest level, the same level as that of the hunting and gathering family, the American family would appear to be at an irreducible level. It is not expected to disappear, so it is going somewhere. It seems there is nowhere to go but up. But up where?

The strain in American society is obviously on the pair-bond. The purpose of the pair-bond is to reproduce and raise offspring. Remove that or replace it, and you've given the pot a heavy stir. Great change is inevitable. The birth rate is way down; divorce is way up; there is a sharp increase in unmarried couples living together. Contraception and available abortion have left sex as pure fun, if that's the way we want it. With practical contraception now available to women for the first time, it can be expected that women will be likely to change more and more rapidly than men.

But there are also forces slowing down change. We are biologically programmed to want children. Few people say they don't want any; many say they're going to limit or postpone children. We also are highly disposed to form pair-bonds; and even with all the sexual experimenting in vogue, stable pair-bonds still form.

For those many who do want and plan children, there is no good substitute for the family as a place to rear them, nor is there any likelihood of a good substitute appearing in the near future.

There is still the historic biology of the sex roles. Both men and women may well be equally good as business executives. But women have tended to be more highly motivated to take care of children, and it does take high motivation.

If the woman is going to be taking care of children, she is not going to be the full-time executive, painter, concert pianist or whatever. Feminists notwithstanding, the biologist and the anthropologist believe there are biologically induced differences of temperament between men and women. Men tend on the average to be more dominant and aggressive. This may well be a matter of chemicals, possibly more testosterone in the average man.

Van den Berghe's analysis makes no attempt to say where the family is going, or what the form will be. On the other hand, there is no Voice of Doom. It is just that the future is murky. But then, the hunters and gatherers probably could not foresee the gardeners. Even today, where different family forms exist almost side-by-side, they probably don't comprehend each other.

Why then should we foresee or understand what may be the next evolutionary development in the family, except to believe there will be some form of family structure?

Since the nuclear family is expected to be with us for some time, it does become wise to take some kinds of action to bolster it. Negative actions, such as gay-bashing and anti-abortion laws, are not likely to have any enduring or positive effect. More promising are positive programs to improve family communication and affection. This is being done.

Coming out of the privatism of the '70s, such disciplines as transactional analysis began to emphasize familial relationships. Even meditation is becoming less a solitary activity and more a group consciousness-sharing experience. Programs are being devised and presented to strengthen the family, often starting from the viewpoint of the individual and arguing that it is to the individual's benefit to smooth out the family situation.

Much of this is clergy-inspired—not hard to understand since Christianity single-mindedly advocates and enforces monogamy. A recent example of a clergy-related program is a television series featuring the Jesuit priest, the Rev. John Powell.

Powell has been best known for such self-realization books as *Why Am I Afraid To Love?* and *Why Am I Afraid To Tell You Who I Am?* Both, it is true, bring the individual into hopefully better relationships, but in the "Family" series, Powell slants directly to the family.

In his opening program, of three, he says:

"I would like to talk to you about messages. I have prepared three programs, one on the messages of the families, and the second program will be on the memories. Memories are so important, aren't they? Memories are born in family interaction. And finally on the meaning of life that can be discovered only in the family."

In his final program, he says:

"It all begins in the family. Everything human is contagious, and it must begin there. We must begin by loving those who are closest to us. Our lives are shaped by those who love us and by those who refuse to love us."

The Rev. Joe Smith, pastor at the downtown Portland St. James Lutheran church, is by no means campaigning as a family activist, but he does have some considered thoughts on the subject. Smith's congregation consists of many corporation families, and he sees them transfer in and out at a dizzying rate.

"The Protestant work ethic does demand mobility for the family," he said. "Obviously that can lead to all kinds of pressures from the outside which can upset the family."

Smith believes the family has lost its sense of ceremony, of celebration, of occasion, and perhaps a renewal of emphasis on that may help bring new interest and vitality to the family.

Nowadays, people look forward to getting through high school; then they look forward to getting married; then what do they have to look forward to? But there is this yearning for more of this mystery. Smith pointed to the nostalgia for Roots—the interest in genealogy. Another symptom: the return of ceremonial pomp in the Ronald Reagan presidency.

Even the renewed interest in creationism may be a search for the story that symbolizes and illuminates our lives.

Smith is by no means discouraged by the present upheaval. "I don't believe we are at a time of doom; we may be at the beginning," he said.

This sense of being on the brink of something is becoming

pervasive. A decade ago, Alvan Toffler spoke of "Future Shock," which really was "Present Shock." Now Toffler is talking about "The Third Wave."

His first wave of change was the transition from hunting and gathering to agrarian society. The second wave was the transition to industrialization. Now comes the third wave. Where is it leading? Toffler, who tends to be an expert at looking off the back of the train, doesn't know.

The yearning for kinship certainly lives. Kurt Vonnegut Jr. for years nursed a pet idea about kinship and developed it in the novel *Slapstick*. He tells about the idea in his preface to *Wampeters, Foma & Granfalloons*.

"My longer-range schemes have to with providing all Americans with artificial extended families of a thousand members or more. Only when we have overcome loneliness can we begin to share wealth and work more fairly. I honestly believe that we will have those families by-and-by, and I hope they will become international."

Here we are, with one in five illiterate, our family structure run full circle to the level of hunters and gatherers—not even quite up to the level of the "village."

All the evidence indicates that the family will survive. It is now functioning at its irreducible minimum. Biological necessity and adaptation will cause it to evolve into some different form, though slowly. Meantime, we are not at the Edge of Doom. We may well be on the threshold of the New Renaissance.

5.10.81

WHO ARE THESE PEOPLE?

Paul Pintarich

What are they waiting for, all these old people who live near our lives? Do they wish to speak to us of how we have changed their world? Do they have dreams and goals and desires we ignore? Maybe they have found the answers to this baffling life, carrying their secrets like faded treasures in their souls, offering them to us with brief and cryptic smiles? Or are they simply tired and waiting to die?

To children they are grandparents with wonderful tales to tell. When we are older they might be parents and we worry about what they're going to do with their remaining years. To others they might be no more than shuffling piles of old clothes and sadness who feed pigeons in the park.

Then it comes to all of us with sickness or good health. The silver hair, the golden door to retirement and suddenly you find yourself in the last depot on the way to death. How do you fill the years that are left?

So sad, too bad and who cares except the old people themselves who live with each other every day. Too proud, maybe, or too sick and confused by a society which no longer needs them.

How wonderful it is to have a crop of young adults ready to replace the old in our society. We turn away from the old and ask the young for contributions to the economy, to culture—to the perpetuation of an idea: Youth, beauty and the happiness of being wrinkle-free.

And an ugly old man with wrinkles shuffles into a personnel office because he just can't live on his meager Social Security check.

"I'm sorry, sir. But even though you are a master mechanic with forty-five years experience and in perfect health we need a younger man." A head-down apology and at home the wife says: "I guess you'll be underfoot all day."

And in many cases now it will be the man and woman sharing a small apartment or a paid-for empty home suddenly too big without children. Here is another sadness of the aged. Where in early rural America families lived together for generations, now we have the departure of the young. Each to his own and no more additions to the family home when the son or daughter marries.

The young as well as the old are victims of the rural-urban migrations. Youth finds better jobs and affluence leads them to the suburbs. Old people are often left in older neighborhoods to welcome urban renewal.

Sophocles said: "No man loves life like him that's growing old." But what is a life to love that moves away or transforms itself before your eyes each day? Even the young sometimes find modern living, its pace, incomprehensible.

It is easy to classify or stereotype the old as "senior citizens," "mature adults," or just plain "old folks." But often, however, we fail to recognize differences among the old themselves. Degrees of wealth, social standing, education—the varied plateaus upon which society places all of us.

For the more fortunate, retirement and old age can offer happiness, desired leisure time and truly comfortable days of living in the sun.

But for others, unfortunately, there are only the depressing, inevitable stages of decline. Lurking are old hotel rooms and inadequate pensions. Nursing homes are often the fate of the sick or senile, and for others the last stop before the grave. And of course there are the rooms in the home of a son or daughter or an old-age residence where people can sit, watching and waiting for each other to die.

Gobbling acres of land and calling to the country's old during recent years have been another "blessing" to the middle- and upper-income groups—the retirement community. Here is advertised heaven on earth. The new Nirvana. A place where silver threads can be spun into dreams of gold. Here also is the place set aside for our old, the reservations, where youth plays no part and the ranks of years are formed up for ping-pong, square dancing and golf.

Though retirement communities vary, most provide amenities to dazzle even the most apathetic senior citizen. Golf is big, some swimming, workshops, craft classes, fishing at some, tours, parties, barbecues at others—house row on row of suburban sameness at many. And always the company of people like other old people.

Where are the children and the young adults? Who is to inspire? What does the man do with the wood lathe when he has been an accountant or insurance salesman all his life and has never had a hobby? Perhaps try painting? Later, bored, walk by the pool, kick a rock and then go back and talk to the wife about getting old and try to avoid the funerals. A silent battle. Like old soldiers. Who went yesterday? The ranks thin out.

Of course it is foolish to say that all old people are unhappy in their own communities. Many have found a new life filled with the companionship of others their own age and many simply do not desire the company of young people or reminders of the life they worked so hard to escape.

Yet there is a question still to be answered. Are the old who live in Senior Citizen Acres motivated by themselves; or are they unknowingly motivated by a youth-oriented society which has told them that that is where they will be happy? Have we unconsciously created "concentration camps" for the old where they will be hidden, not to remind us of our own inevitable fate?

Away from the suburban retirement community, in the cities, remain the hangers-on, so to speak, the ones left in homes which were once part of a comfortable neighborhood. Perhaps there is a little money coming in; but what if a man or woman wants to work? They must fight the prejudices of the young again. Having faced mandatory retirement, where can they go? If they have developed no hobbies or interests outside of their life's work, they have the alternatives of either sitting and staring or talking to someone who has heard the stories many times before.

The young have the responsibility of recognizing the old as individuals; as personalities rather than as just being old. They have much to offer, these old people.

On celebrating his 90th birthday, Oliver Wendell Holmes said: "The race is over, but the work never is done while the power to work remains...For to live is to function, that is all there is to living."

When we listen to an old person for awhile, then walk away, smiling and saying: "He's just an old duffer. He's lived his life and has a lot of good stories," we never listen beyond what we want to hear. The words were heard by our ears but we didn't take the time to put them in our hearts. The old have lived life. Many have seen or been through it all, others a great part of it, and they have survived and are still around to tell about it. Lessons, and we laugh and walk away.

The skin may be clear as parchment, but old fingers are still often clever to turn screws or build a fine piece of furniture. Many sharp minds are still able to contribute by teaching when the hands or eyes are weak.

Perhaps it is time we turned from the loud voices of the young and listened more closely to the whispers of the old. Can we learn to see them—not simply as grampas and grandmas, pigeon-feeders and winos or golf-playing corpses, but as people with names and skills and lives of their own?

Through medical science and technology we have created a surplus of years. We are keeping ourselves alive longer, yet, at the same time, we are ignoring the product of our achievements. Old people today, an increasing number of them living into their 80s and 90s, are crowding into our culture to be seen. We take care of them, perhaps well, perhaps not so well, until they die; shuddering as we do so, seeing in their silent faces mirrored reflections of Dorian Gray.

We will all be old and await the same fate—whether old age means pleasure or simply a bland interlude before the grave. What we do now, how we perceive and treat our old, however, may someday determine how we will finish our lives.

In his work, *Balthazar*, the English novelist Lawrence Durrell said it so beautifully: "First the young, like vines, climb up the dull supports of their elders who feel their fingers upon them, soft and tender; then the old climb down the lovely supporting bodies of the young into their proper deaths."

4.27.69

EXCERPTS FROM NOTEWORTHY STORIES

Breaking the Bond: The Need For Alternatives To Marriage
by Barbara J. Murphy
10.21.73

"Men and women are no longer content to act merely according to custom, hoping in the end some meaning will emerge. What they are really asking for are more flexible roles in society which give individuals more of a chance to develop and utilize their potentials than the traditional marriage structure with its dependence on the dominant male role has afforded. This may or may not result in other than traditional living arrangements. It most assuredly will involve other than traditional premises on which these arrangements are founded."

Our Children: Lost or Thrown Away?
by S. G. Radhuber
12.12.76

"We are changing. What our society will be like when our traditional institutions are gone I don't know. Unless we are intelligent and vigilant, however, we might be heading toward a chaos that will make the days of Nero Claudius Caesar seem like the Rose Festival. Our passionate commitment to freedom and free enterprise has spawned ugliness, pornography, the breakdown of the family, violence, disrespect for authority. Every attempt at reform brings about an ugly counter stroke. Adults are becoming narcissistic children, and the children are becoming wide-eyed realists. As a society we have, at this stage, accepted the 19th century view of man as a product of evolution—an animal in the most pejorative sense—and we seem willing to live with that idea. But we have at the same time rejected morality, restraint and decorum, and somehow we have managed to create a society which is brutalizing, pornographic, and self-indulgent. And for this, we can't blame our children."

A Report on Family Violence
by Joseph B. Trainer, MD
2.13.77

"The proximity, the sense of license, the prior environment and the close emotional relation to family members make intrafamily violence the most probable in a violent society and in a violent species.

"What we can do about it is something different. As of now, serious antisocial behavior, especially violent behavior, results in the offender being shunted into some sort of custodial care institution labeled either a prison or a mental hospital. For the most part, no adequate study is made of the nature of the disorder and the undiagnosed, untreated individual is warehoused for a time, then released perhaps to the further hazard of the family or society."

The Traditional Family: Requiem or Revival?
by David Shetzline
5.10.81

"As Oregonians tighten expectations for the 1980s, is it wise to suspect that the traditional family will reappear? Certainly not. Gone with spruce shakes, backyard windmills, butter churns. And yet...

"Take Beaver Creek in Lincoln County. Barely 15 miles from its headwaters in old and second-growth timber, this drainage is celebrated locally as watering one of the most picturesque of the coastal valleys. Although only three or four families make a living without drawing wages from their mailbox or working out, a third generation of homesteaders remembers when a dozen times that many folk hand-built their own places and nurtured families of five to seven children who shared chores, raised barns, milked cows and milled timber before resettling to city life in the decades between World War II and the last of Vietnam.

"...Unspoken things are remembered, too. Not because they were embarrassing or disgraceful or tragic. But they are pieces of a family's private traditions. Yet the steelhead still run, the bear peevishly feed on skunk cabbage, the coyote yet howl on the ridges—if only once or twice a winter—and new generations move in to build and raise their own families. Has the traditional life already returned with the challenge of self-help, alternative energy, backyard survival gardens, personal and moral reaffirmation?"

four:

Sports

"The Blazers: It's Been Quite A Year"
by Larry Colton
"Portland was no longer satisfied to just be in the playoffs. The
world championship had become a real possibility."

"Thoughts And Thumps At Ringside"
by Gerry Pratt
"Artie keeps pushing that long left hand into the other kid's
face. It isn't hurting him bad in the sense of the fight
game, but it isn't doing his ego any good, either."

"The Last Slow Dance"
by Charles Deemer
"It takes the pitcher some ten seconds to throw the ball,
which more often than not is taken by the batter for a ball
or strike. This, baseball fans, is the most action you'll see in
the next half-minute or more. Which is baseball's advantage!"

THE BLAZERS: IT'S BEEN QUITE A YEAR

Larry Colton

As the crowd of 12,736 excited Trail Blazer fans file their way into Portland's Memorial Coliseum for the Blazers' afternoon playoff game with the Denver Nuggets, a middle-aged man exits the antique show in the exhibit hall adjoining the coliseum. Startled to see all the people, the man asks, "What's going on in the big building today?"

"The Trail Blazers are having a playoff game," a fan replies.

"Oh yes," the man responds, nodding his head. "I heard something about that."

It is pretty hard for anyone in Portland not to have heard something about the Trail Blazers this year. From Maurice Lucas' game-winning windmill slam dunk over Kareem Abdul-Jabbar in the team's first exhibition game way back in October, to the current battle with Philadelphia for the National Basketball Association championship, the Blazers have captured a sports following unparalleled in Portland's history.

For the Blazer organization—owners as well as players— it's the end of a long and sometimes turbulent seven-year struggle to make it to the coveted NBA playoffs. During those years, the Blazers were compiling, among other things: The worst record in the NBA, three ex-coaches, Sidney Wicks' inflated red headbands, assorted problems with Bill Walton and a growing number of disgruntled fans, impatient for a winner.

Playoff tickets have become worth their weight in coffee; throngs pack the airport to greet the team; the mayor is a wide-eyed visitor in the Blazer locker room, and every Blazer victory is a front-page headline.

Blazermania, playoff fever, Rip City hysteria: Call it what you like, but everyone seems to know something about the Blazers.

But do they? Let's see what you know about the Blazers and the NBA playoffs.

Trivimania Quiz

1. How many of the Blazers live on the east side of the Willamette River?
2. Match the Blazer with his transportation.

    A. Bill Walton   1. Chevrolet
    B. Lionel Hollins   2. Porsche
    C. Bob Gross   3. Datsun 280-Z
    D. Lloyd Neal   4. Cadillac
    E. Wally Walker   5. Mercedes

3. True or False? The Blazers' 6'1" guard, Dave Twardzik, can dunk.
4. Who scored more points in their high school career, Blazer reserve center Robin Jones or Portland Mayor Neil Goldschmidt?
5. Blazer coach, Dr. Jack Ramsay, wrote a book titled: A) Pressure Basketball B) The Wizard of the Willamette C) Call Me Coach D) I See By Your Outfit.
6. The average profit for a scalped ticket at the first Chicago playoff game was: A) $25 B) $3.40 per hour C) Illegal.
7. The major issue in the referees' strike was: A) Money B) Pension C) Tenure D) New whistles.
8. What Portland high school did Blazer executive vice-president Harry Glickman graduate from? A) Lincoln B) Grant C) Catlin Gabel D) Failed to graduate
9. What did Wally Walker eat for breakfast on the morning of the fourth Laker game? A) Fruit Loops and Tang B) Scrambled eggs, toast, orange juice C) Avocado sandwich, sprouts, carrot juice D) Who cares?
10. In Blazer jargon, what is an Ice Blue secret?

The answers to the above questions are all included in the following account of the Blazers' drive for the championship.

On a small strip of grass located between the Coliseum and the Broadway Bridge, Bill Walton sets down his 10-speed bicycle and then lies back to take advantage of the warm spring sunshine on the day before the Blazers' first playoff game with the Chicago Bulls, at that time the hottest team in the NBA. Dressed only in a pair of cutoff jeans and sandals, Walton ignores the honking and gawking of passing motorists as he recalls some of the turmoil of his first year in Portland—a period punctuated with assorted injuries, FBI hassles, a falling-out with his advisor and problems with a press that he had never really been exposed to before, even though his picture had been on the cover of *Sports Illustrated* when he was only 18.

"It was difficult for me when I first moved to Portland," Walton recalled. "It's tough to move to a completely new environment. Everyone knew me, but I did not know anyone. Also, the rain was getting to me; I was used to the warm winters in California."

But the horrors of that first year—the baskets of hate mail, the charges of malingering, the post-LA blues—all seemed distant as Walton relaxed, soaking up the sunshine on the day before the start of the 1977 NBA playoffs. "I love it here in Portland now, especially when the weather is nice like this. I doubt if I'll move back to California. This is my home. San Diego was okay, but about the only part of LA that I enjoyed was the basketball at UCLA.

"As far as our chances in the playoffs are concerned," he said, choosing his words, "I won't make any predictions, but I'm very optimistic. We have a very balanced team. That's what is so good about us; you never know who is going to be the star from game to game.

"In the NBA," he continued, "the best team is going to win. Chicago is a very hot team right now...but so are we."

As Walton got up to leave, he brushed the grass off his back before mounting his bicycle. "The high point of my career," he concluded, shielding his eyes from the sun, "will be when we win the NBA championship."

He paused for a second and then added with a wide smile

before pedaling off, "This is a great way to make a living; playing basketball and enjoying the sun."

At the Blazers' shooting practice at the Coliseum the next morning, the day of their first game against the Bulls, the team appeared relaxed. Radio announcer Bill Schonely stood under the basket at one end of the court and retrieved free throws for Maurice Lucas while Lionel Hollins and rookie Wally Walker (the darling of the Portland crowd), played one-on-one at the other end, closely watched by Ramsay. When Hollins sank four straight shots, Walker countered by kicking the ball halfway up the empty coliseum.

Outside the arena, as the fans began to arrive for the game, the scalpers, some of whom waited in the early morning ticket lines for five hours to purchase their tickets, openly negotiated their sales. Two $9.50 seats were sold for a total of $36, which figured out to be a $3.40 hourly wage for the scalper.

As Bob Gross and Lionel Hollins say in their omnipresent TV commercial for Chevrolet (both men drive Datsun 280-Zs), "It's a whole new ball game."

Inside the coliseum, the Trail Blazer fans were on their feet, giving the team a standing ovation as the Blazers broke their huddle and headed for the tipoff. Maurice Lucas sank the first shot, jumped up in the air in the excitement and the Blazers were on their way.

But three quick fouls called on Walton by the "scabs," as a courtside observer heard more than one angry player call the inexperienced referees substituting for the striking NBA refs, and suddenly the Blazers' chances and the NBA's rejection of the demands of the striking referees looked bad.

Maurice Lucas took charge of the game, however, muscling in 29 points, and the Blazers' baptism into the NBA playoffs was successful, 96–83. Talk of a lack of playoff experience was quickly silenced.

In the second game in Chicago, an ear-splitting crowd of 22,000 along with 1) some questionable officiating, 2) the ejection of Herm Gilliam and 3) the play of a Blazer that got away, Mickey Johnson, all contributed to the Bulls' 107–104 victory to set the stage for the third and deciding game in Portland.

In the final game, when Twardzik, Walton and Lucas all fouled out in the fourth quarter, the Blazers chances did not look good. But with Walton standing up on the sidelines the entire last five minutes, hands placed nervously behind his head, exhorting his teammates, the Blazers were able to win the game and the series on a dramatic 20-foot jumper by Lionel Hollins with 15 seconds to go. Coupled with Bob Gross' career-high 26 points and some clutch play off the bench by Robin Jones, the Blazers had eliminated the Bulls and earned the right to meet jumping David Thompson and the Denver Nuggets in the quarterfinals.

In the jubilant Blazer locker room after the game, tennis-shoe-clad Mayor Neil Goldschmidt (who scored more points at South Eugene High than Robin Jones did in his high school career), was all smiles as he offered congratulations to the victorious Blazers.

The Chicago series had produced a different high-scorer for the Blazers every game: Lucas, Walton, then Gross. Walton's pre-Playoff comment about a different hero every game was looking accurate.

Following the last game of the Chicago series, the Bulls' coach, Ed Badger, said "I think the Blazers will beat Denver and go on to beat Los Angeles for the Western Conference title. I think we were the only team in the conference that could beat them."

Blazer coach Jack Ramsay said of the Chicago series, "I think our young team may have gained more maturity from that series than anything else all season."

The young Blazers showed that maturity in their first game in Denver, winning 101–100 on a clutch basket by Maurice Lucas with 11 seconds to go. When Denver tried to get off a last-second shot to win the game, nobody wanted the ball, and the Nuggets had suddenly lost the home court advantage.

In the second game, however, Denver parlayed 39 free throw attempts and center Dan Issel's 36 points into a 121–110 victory to send the playoff back to Portland tied at one game apiece.

Asked later if he thought the high altitude in Denver had any effect on performance, Walton replied, "I'm not sure, but I did see Twardzik dunking in warm-ups and I'd never seen him do that before."

When the Blazers arrived at the Coliseum following an early morning flight from Denver, they showed the effects of the travel and the extremely physical first two games in Denver. Twardzik and Lucas stayed in the locker room to tend to their aches and pains while the rest of the team listlessly went through a short workout. The only people on the court going at full speed were Barry Weinberg, son of Lawrence Weinberg, one of the Blazers' owners, cavorting with the team, and Wally Walker, usually the last Blazer to leave the practice court.

"I haven't played enough to be tired," said the personable Walker, who was once accused of committing a foul even before getting out of his Porsche in the parking lot.

"I'm disappointed at not getting to play more," Walker said. "But I realize that my play has been erratic this year. I think I can be a good NBA ballplayer, however. Hopefully, I'll get to play more to prove what I can do."

The next day, at the start of game three, public address announcer Jimmy Jones interrupted the bedlam of the crowd to announce the starting lineups. Lucas went up and down the line of Blazers, slapping each man while the Denver players were being introduced. Everybody in the building was on their feet.

Two minutes into the game, non-striking referee Richie Powers whistled a foul on Walton and a cascade of boos rocked the Coliseum.

"Whistle Issel, you jerk!" screamed an irate fan in section 61. The Blazer fans' patience for the referees was wearing thin. In the first five playoff games, the Blazers had been to the freethrow line 103 times, as compared to 163 times for their opponents.

But the Blazers didn't let the referees bother them as they won, 110–106, sparked by a combined 53 points from Walton and Lucas, a great job off the bench by Gilliam, Neal and Walker, and a half-court swisher by Hollins at the end of the third quarter that ignited the crowd and got the highly excitable Robin Jones so keyed that he strayed from the Blazer huddle to do a mini-war dance near the free-throw line.

The following morning in the Blazer office in the Lloyd Building, Harry Glickman smiled as he talked about the team's 2–1 lead in the series. "I'd still consider the season a success even if we lost the rest of our games...but nobody is going to beat us three straight."

Glickman quickly stopped smiling, however, as he changed the subject to the referees' strike. "Their timing is atrocious. They could have waited until after the playoffs.

"The major issue is not the money, although it's a factor. The issue that's holding up a settlement is tenure. Hell, if they were to get their way, a ref could report 50 pounds overweight and still be guaranteed of his job. It's ridiculous."

While Glickman's anger over the timing of the strike may be well-founded, the NBA's failure to negotiate a settlement indicated either a lack of regard for both the players and the fans or a poor negotiating team. It should be pointed out, however, that the NBA Players Association did not bring any pressure on the NBA to end the strike, failing even to make a strong public statement calling for the end of the dispute.

The referees' strike was not the only off-court problem that Glickman, a Lincoln High graduate and the man responsible for bringing the Blazers to Portland, had to deal with. His decision not to televise some of the home games created widespread criticism. KPTV and the Blazer office were flooded with calls from hostile fans, unable to get tickets and demanding to know why they couldn't see the sold-out games.

"I realize it's an unpopular decision," Glickman said, raising his voice slightly. "But there's just too many factors involved why we can't do it. It would take 30 minutes for me to explain them all. For one thing, it wouldn't be fair to the people who paid good money to buy a ticket. And yesterday, when the game was on TV, there were 300 no-shows. It just would not be good business."

Television or no television, referees or no referees, the players and coaches were all saying that game number four against Denver was going to be the key game of the series, an invocation that seemed to precede every playoff game.

On the morning of the crucial game, Jack Ramsay arrived at the Blazers' office precisely at 9 a.m., dressed in a sweatsuit and tennis shoes. Inside his office, decorated with a Leroy Neiman painting and a plaque that advises "Bald men make great lovers," Ramsay shuffled through the stack of mail on his desk as he talked about his coaching style and the Blazer team.

"My job is to direct the team, to give them the type of game that best fits the talent available. I'm not running a democracy; my job is to win games, not to see that everybody plays.

"Everybody has played this year, however, and that helps. There's been no moaning and bitching. The players on this team are all team-oriented; it is a very cohesive club and that started in our first meetings last summer. I've never been associated with a better team.

"When I'm not using somebody, I try to communicate to them the reason why. For instance, I haven't used Larry Steele much in the past couple of games because he's playing lousy, quite frankly. I talked with Larry yesterday and told him just that. I also talked with Wally. They understand."

For Ramsay, who holds a doctorate in education and has taught classes in both high school and college, in addition to having written a book titled *Pressure Basketball*, this is his 20th year as coach. "The high point of my coaching career," he said, echoing Walton, "will be when we win the NBA championship."

When asked what player he would like to acquire if given the chance, Ramsay replied without hesitation, "Pete Maravich. I really admire him; he plays our style, very unselfish. I also have tremendous respect for (Kareem) Abdul-Jabbar (of Los Angeles), but we already have a center."

Good news prior to the start of the fourth game came when it was announced that the referees' walkout had ended. When referees Manny Sokol and Earl Strom entered the arena, they were given an ovation, prompting one fan, who had paid $40 to a scalper, to comment. "Whoever thought I'd be paying out this kind of money to come in here and applaud these turkeys?"

But that fan got at least part of his money's worth that evening as the Blazers, after blowing a 13-point lead, held on to score a 105–96 victory, led by Bob Gross' 25 points.

Ramsay gave the team the day off following its fourth game victory, and the players enjoyed the respite from their very physical battle with the Nuggets. Walton took advantage of the free time to try a little fishing in the Columbia. He was skunked, but when asked what he would have done if he had caught a fish, considering his vegetarian diet, he replied with a chuckle, "I've never caught a fish in my life, so how would I know?"

The next day, it was back to practice as usual at the Mittleman Jewish Community Center, but Walton was excused from participating in order to rest a sore toe. After practice, as Walton carefully eased his new Mercedes, which was parked next to Lloyd Neal's Cadillac, out of the parking lot, he looked ahead to the possibility of meeting the Los Angeles Lakers or the Golden State Warriors in the semifinals.

"Of all the teams in the league, LA, Golden State and Denver are my favorite teams to play, because they play my style of basketball. For obvious reasons," he added with a smile, "it would be more fun if we played Los Angeles."

When Walton pulled his car to a stop in front of his rented house in Northwest Portland (all of the Blazers live on the west side), he was greeted in the middle of the street by Adam, his blond curlyheaded 1½-year-old-son. After warning Adam of the dangers of being in the street, Bill swooped him up, kissed him and then placed him on his shoulders for a ride to the house. Asked if he ever changed the diapers, Bill replied with a laugh, "Oh, maybe a few times, but I have other jobs. I'm not saying that I believe in a division of labor, but…"

In game number five in Denver, the Blazers lost in overtime, but perhaps more importantly, they lost their kamikaze guard Dave Twardzik indefinitely with a severely sprained ankle, causing concern in the Blazer camp.

But lickity brindle rookie Johnny Davis, who had played only sparingly the last two months of the season, responded by equaling his career high of 25 points to lead the Blazers to their easiest victory, 108–92, sending them into the semifinals.

Davis allegedly came to the attention of the Blazers' scouting corps last year through a word-of-mouth recommendation to Blazer assistant coach Tom Meschery from a Portland historian, John Strawn, who had heard about Davis from a friend back east.

In the Blazer locker room after the game, the Mayor was there again to congratulate the team, and Ramsay, dressed in his canary yellow pants, told his interviewers that it was a total team victory, with Davis and Larry Steele playing key roles.

With the Blazers' triumph over Denver, further credence was given to Walton's pre-playoff statement about the balanced attack of the Blazers. Nevertheless, odds makers (who the heck is Jimmy the Greek?) listed Portland as an 8–5 underdog to the Lakers and Kareem Abdul-Jabbar, the winningest team and the most valuable player in the NBA.

It never rains in Southern California…it only pours. Man, it pours.

It rained in Los Angeles on the morning of the first semifinal game between the Blazers and the Lakers, causing one drenched Laker fan to moan, "This rain is going to give Portland the home-court advantage tonight."

Inside the Forum, out of the rain, the Blazers were going through their noon shooting practice. They appeared more tense and stiff than usual. There was laughter, as the team went through its fast break drills, but it seemed nervous.

As round one of the Big Matchup (Abdul-Jabbar vs. Walton, Lucas, Hollins, et. al.) neared, the stylish Laker fans began filing into the Forum, looking like they had just stepped out of a commercial for Southern California living. The parking lot was filled with row after row of expensive gas-guzzlers.

The Blazers were introduced to the late-arriving crowd, with a smattering of boos reserved for Walton. Then the lights were turned off and the spotlight was turned on, as the Lakers entered the arena to the rhythmic beat of a Stevie Wonder song, chosen from the personal tape collection of Laker forward Cazzie Russell, who orchestrates the Forum pre-game music. Overhead, a glittering Hollywood light show danced on the ceiling.

The introductions were about the last thing the Laker crazies had to cheer about that evening as Blazer guards Hollins and Davis took the Forum freeway via the Walton overpass to drive past the star-struck Angelenos, 121–109.

Beep beep zoom, and away went the devastating Blazer fast break, with four Blazer starters scoring 20 or more points, Lucas being tops with 28. The Lakers' last hope disappeared when Johnny Davis didn't hurt himself when he hit his head on the backboard going in for a stuff shot.

After the game, in a conference room set up for the large press corps assembled to cover the series, Laker coach Jerry West told his interviewers that he had been saying all year that he thought Portland might have the best talent in the league.

When Walton entered the conference room, he suspiciously eyed the gathering of 30 writers, all eager to find out his feelings about round one of his ballyhooed duel with Abdul-Jabbar. For Walton, dealing with the media has become a necessary evil that he considers "part of the whole trip" of being a basketball star.

Although Bill gets along well with the Portland press, his relationship with the national media has not exactly been a honeymoon, especially during his hectic first year. Basically a very private person, Walton had trouble dealing with his sudden exposure to the probing press, eager to find out his views on everything from the skyhook to hamburgers to Patty Hearst. Bill had majored in history and basketball at UCLA, not speech and drama, so it was understandable that he was uneasy with the press.

Some of the blame for that has to go to John Wooden, Bill's coach at UCLA. Although his policy of shielding his college ballplayers from the press was well-intentioned, Wooden might have served both Walton and Jabbar better by giving them gradual exposure to the press in order to better prepare them for the media deluge they were certain to face as pros. Walton and Jabbar were enigmas to a voracious press by graduation day.

Bill's relationship with the fourth estate has improved this year, however. "The writers know me better now, and I know them better," he explains.

Improved relations with the media does not mean total harmony, however. Walton will not talk about anything other than basketball with writers he does not know. Understandably, he often acts bored or irritated at the constant imposition and endless stream of inane questions about his diet, his health or his moves to the left. "How do you feel, Bill?" he was asked for the jillionth time. "I'm going to be what I'm going to be," he responded.

As Walton addressed the collection of reporters after that first game in Los Angeles, he looked frustrated by the ordeal, giving terse answers in a low voice. A heavy-set Los Angeles writer in the back of the room shook his head.

On Sunday afternoon, the day of game number two, a tornado whipped through a section of nearby Long Beach, causing extensive damage to a hospital and a franchised restaurant. At the same time at the Forum in Inglewood, a whirlwind was blowing through the Los Angeles backcourt, also causing heavy damage to a franchise.

Led by tricky contortions of Herm Gilliam (alias Squirmin' Herman, Trickster or Hair Herman) and 31 points and eight steals from Hollins, the Blazers rode the Train to an exciting 99–97 victory, completing the impossible—a sweep of the Lakers in Boss Angeles.

After the game, Ramsay talked of the rare collection of unselfish people on the team. "They are so young to be doing what they are doing," he said, his voice cracking with emotion. "I am very proud of them."

After the two games in Los Angeles, neither of which was sold out, Bob Gross, who went to high school and college in the LA area, commented on the Laker crowd: "They were low keyed; they never seemed to get going."

Young Johnny Davis, who wasn't even old enough to go out and have a beer with the guys when the season started, said that he felt the contingent of 200 or so Blazer boosters who had made the trip to LA were louder than the Laker crowd. One LA fan tried to blame the empty seats and the subdued nature of the crowd on the wet weather, a rationalization that wasn't likely to hold water with the Portland fans.

Following the Blazers' stunning two-game sweep in Los Angeles, the team was given a rousing reception at the airport upon its return to Portland. Everyone was caught up in the first-degree terminal Blazermania that had gripped the city. Portland was no longer satisfied to just be in the playoffs. The world championship had become a real possibility.

National attention was now being focused on the team. Brent "Call him Mountainman" Mussberger and CBS were now giving maximum exposure to the team. Press people from all over the country were coming out of the woodwork, making Blazer publicity director John White's job a nightmare. There were more women in the Blazer locker room, taking notes, snapping pictures and recording conversations, than there were towels to go around.

With all of the excitement about the Blazers' success, the anticipation for round three in Portland was at a high as the scalpers gathered in front of the Coliseum prior to tipoff. A new city ordinance to prevent the reselling of tickets at more than face value was having little effect. Tickets were selling for an average of $50, with one person shelling out $75 for a standing-room-only ticket.

Another ticket buyer, finding it difficult to make a deal, desperately offered to trade his ticket to the sold-out Pink Floyd rock concert for a ticket to game three. "You're kidding, of course?" another fan interjected, incredulously. "That would be the worst deal since Moses Malone."

Inside the arena, the crowd was buzzing, awaiting the arrival of its heroes. The much larger Forum seemed like a morgue compared to the cozy confines of the Coliseum. When coach Ramsay and his assistant, Jack McKinney, walked across the floor to take their place on (or near) the Blazer bench, they were given a standing ovation. McKinney was to remark after the game, "When the crowd gave Jack and me that ovation I was wishing that there was some way that I could acknowledge the warmth

of the crowd without looking like a hot dog. It was a very grati-
fying feeling."

With the crowd screaming its approval, the Blazers won
game three, 102–97, as a palooka named Ford couldn't box Lucas
off the boards and Walton went on a 14-point scoring spree in
the fourth quarter, highlighted by a flying stuff shot over Jabbar
following a hustling save by Lucas. The Lakers were now one
game away from their summer vacation.

With the Blazers up 3–0, there was some concern about the
team becoming overconfident. When the Blazers arrived for practice at the Mittleman Jewish Community Center the day before
game four, just as ex-Blazer Geoff Petrie was completing a workout of his own, the players were loose, providing a stark contrast to the tension before game one. After the practice was over,
Ramsay termed it a lousy workout.

Nevertheless, the Blazers were all business as they took the
floor for the start of the fourth game. The fans, the chosen and
the beautiful of Portland, were in a frenzy, applauding everything that moved in a Blazer uniform.

While Walton and Jabbar were neutralizing each other underneath, the rest of the Blazers were demonstrating the finer
points of team basketball to capture a 105–101 victory and qualify
for the finals of the basketball championship of the world.

In the dressing room after the game, the Blazers broke out a
limited supply of champagne to celebrate their greatest victory
ever. The locker room scene was familiar. There was laughter.
There was backslapping. There was Goldschmidt, discussing the
politics of power with Lucas. Freddie Brown of the Seattle Sonics
(what was it Slick Watts said about Walton and the Blazers?)
was there to congratulate former teammate Gilliam.

And Ramsay was there, saying that he was pleased, but not
surprised at the Blazer accomplishment. When asked what the
key to the series was, he replied, "We could not have won the
series without Bill. Nobody has ever played Kareem as tough as
Bill did this series. He was magnificent. If I was going to start a
basketball team, I would begin with Bill Walton. He can do so
many things."

Larry Steele, who has been through the lean years with the Blazers, sat in front of his locker after the game and talked about his feelings about the victory and the whole spirit of Blazermania. "It's the ultimate basketball experience," he said. "The community and the team working together."

Lucas thought about his feelings for a second and then offered, "There's a lot of ways to explain it, but beautiful is a hell of a way."

The Blazers had eight days before the start of the championship series with Philadelphia. Consequently, they appeared rested and relaxed as they prepared to work out at the coliseum two days prior to their departure for Philadelphia. Lloyd Neal (nicknamed Ice by his teammates) and Larry Steele (nicknamed Blue) talked privately at midcourt (an Ice Blue secret?) as Hollins, Walker and Lucas all rehearsed their moves for next season's slam-dunk contest.

Much has been said in praise of the cohesive, team-oriented nature of the young Blazers. On the other hand, the Philadelphia 76ers have been maligned all year for their one-on-one style of basketball. The press and fans have reacted as if the team was supposed to win every game. Coach Gene Shue has been criticized by many, including the wife of the team's star, Julius Erving ("Doctor J"). Dissension was supposed to be the password of the Philly dressing room.

Walton thinks the 76ers have received a bad rap, however. "You don't make it to the NBA finals without working together as a team. Philadelphia has a very fine team and they have an excellent coach."

The 76ers proved Walton right in game one, defeating the turnover-plagued Blazers, 107–101. Doctor J scored 33 points and guard Doug Collins added 30, outscoring all of the Blazer guards. Walton's new haircut was not a factor, unless you're superstitious. Regardless of the outcome of the championship series, the young Blazers have provided the fans of Portland with an exciting year of basketball. They are a team with great future. *(Note: the Blazers, of course, won the championship.)*

For those who believe in such stuff, there is also evidence

that the Blazers might be a team of destiny. Consider the following:

In a scholarly book about Northwest history, *Flood Tide of Empire*, is a story taken in part from the journals of Lewis and Clark and another explorer named, ironically, David Thompson.

The journals relate how the explorers encountered an Indian chief in Oregon. The chief was accompanied by a man described as "...about 25 years of age, with long red hair, fair skin and a partially freckled face. He is slender and remarkably well made and at least half white."

On the redhead's arm was tattooed the name of his father, an English sailor who had deserted his ship and had lived with the Indians. The father's name was Jack Ramsay.

The final twist from this historical data comes in the footnoted bibliography. It seems that part of the research came from a book titled *The Doctor in Oregon*.

5.29.77

THOUGHTS AND THUMPS AT RINGSIDE

Gerry Pratt

East side, west side, all around the town. What a strange way to begin a prize fight story. Jimmy Cannon did it. He wrote that great column about the second or the third Rocky Graziano-Tony Zale fight.

The scheme was that as Graziano came dancing down the aisle between the seats toward the ring the organ would play the song of New York. And as Tony Zale, the Man of Steel from Gary, Indiana, came into the ring, they would play "Away back home to Indiana."

Memory leaves me on how Cannon worked it out, but Graziano was scheduled to be first into the ring. The organ began with "East side, west side, all around the town..." Only somebody missed a cue and instead it was Tony Zale coming through the crowd. The wheezing Coliseum organ came to a grinding halt, then began picking up the pieces by swinging into "Away back home to Indiana."

And that's the way Tony Zale wrote the fight, taking the Rock by Rock punches through the early rounds, working hard on the midsection, digging into the body, shaking off the rocks in Graziano's fist—three, four rounds of them, then slowly cutting Graziano down. The fight followed the musical script and when Cannon did it on paper, even from three thousand or so miles away, you could feel the leather bunching up under your ribs as Zale dug away, softening up the belly, raising tender, red welts around the kidneys and the round-by-round strength was beat from Graziano's body.

They fought two or three times, maybe four, one winning

one match, the other the next. I am not enough of a fight buff any more to give you the details of who won which; I was just one of the radio ringsiders pushing for a place close to the Philco to hear Don Dumphie and Bill Corum take you into the center of the ring. They could do it so the lights squinted in your eyes and the smoke filtered out through the miles. It was all there.

Those were the days of things like "Gillette Blue Blades, with the sharpest edges ever honed," days of Saddler and Pep, Gavilan and Marcel Cerdan for a fight or two and Zivic and Arturo Gudoy and the great stoic Brown Bomber. Even in delayed broadcasts they stirred something in the angry gut of a short-changed world.

It comes back to me now, the whole fist-in-the-palm excitement as Dumphie painted the man on the ropes, taking lefts and rights to the midsection. Those were the days when Corum would announce with Hemingway viciousness that disguises itself as manliness: "He was saved by the bell." And nobody ever asked, "For what?"

The Federal Trade Commission would want to take a good measured look at your edges today if you went on the air with the line about "the sharpest edges ever honed." And mankind today seems somewhat reluctant to pay two guys to fight each other like they did back in those days. Muhammad Ali and Joe Frazier, you say? It has been a slow evolution, but that exhibition they are talking about somewhere in deepest Africa will have to make up in rhetoric for what the fight game once was.

It has come slowly, that evolution from bare knuckles in fifty rounds or more (or until one man was beaten out of his body) to the fifteen-rounders with the light gloves where you could knock a man down as many times as he could get up, one round or fifteen. Now it's the automatic eight count, the heavier gloves and something else, the growing suspicion that the whole thing, the "manly art of self-defense," like throwing Christians to the lions, ultimately does more harm to those who sit and pay to watch than it does to those who bruise and bloody themselves for the entertainment dollar at the end.

Why all this today, now? Well, the Canadian kids were in

town one night recently for the amateur fights. Three rounds a match. The skinny-legged kids with big leather pouches tied to their dukes, head gear and all. And for ten bucks, the money to go to the Olympic boxing team, you got a seat close enough to let you hear the leather smack against the bare cheeks and belly muscles.

There was something—maybe the "Johnny Addie" type voice announcing, "In this cornah, weighing one hunret and tirty pounds…"—that brought back the fight memories of Zale and Graziano, brought back "Miss Gladys Gooding and our National Anthem," the flag as a prelude to the American scene. It was there again at the amateur bouts all right. The stirring of the old "Saturday night fights are on the air…"

Two skinny kids came out of their corners; Corum and Dumphie would have them "dancing out…" One with a quick left hand stuffed it into the other kid's face. Shock, surprise and a little trickle of blood happened all at once. Suddenly, the kid with the glow in his face again and again seemed smaller and skinnier than the other kid. The losers always do.

"Belt him, Artie," a young boy in the seat next to mine hollered. "Belt him, Artie. Knock him into next week," someone else hollered from across the ring.

And slap, slap. Artie keeps pushing that long left hand into the other kid's face. It isn't hurting him bad in the sense of the fight game, but it isn't doing his ego any good, either. The smaller kid gets anxious after a while and lets go with a Gavilan bolo punch that sails clear over the skinny kid's head, and wham, Artie lets him have a right smack in his face for his troubles. The kid lands on the seat of his pants. The referee starts cleaning the gloves against his shirt and looking into the kid's eyes. That's sort of the five-second encephalogram, the fight game's version of checking you for brain damage. At the count of eight the referee steps aside and the kid starts getting Artie's left in the kisser again. Only now he is backing up and he keeps backing up for the rest of the fight, slapping his fists together and jumping back out of the way when he can.

Artie could have been out of the Bronx, he's so instinctive

about what he wants and whap, whap, he keeps tagging the kid through round two and three. The youngster in the seat next to me has stopped yelling, "Belt him, Artie." Maybe he has seen something that makes him wonder what he's cheering for. Anyway, another seat away, his old man has taken up the chant and he's yelling for both of them, "Belt him, Artie, belt him."

There was a man to lead the loser away, resplendent with a silver medal on a red, white and blue ribbon; the winner got a gold medal on the same kind of ribbon. A girl in a short skirt had slipped between the ropes to hand the medals on the boys. The loser laughed. It was a laugh that was hard to come by and it stopped as quickly as it started, even as some guy in a suit was roughing up his hair in a "good old boy" fashion, like you do for a good bird dog coming out through the thin ice. Everybody loves a good loser.

Two more kids were getting into the ring then and the popcorn tasted salty and soft. The skinny kid with the blood on his nose slipped through the ropes in the undistinguished fashion of the loser and walked toward the dressing room. And the announcer began giving the pitch once more: "In this cornah, weighing one hunret…" and the last echoes of Bill Corum's Kentucky Derby masculinity came rasping through the speaker system of my memory, trying to make a hero out of a prize fighter for taking a beating "like a man." All of that was apparently of another time. Gatsby clothes, flapper dresses, bell bottoms, they have all come back. But the fight game? It's better left in mind's eyes, like it was. The audience has aged.

7.14.74

THE LAST SLOW DANCE

Charles Deemer

The Portland Urban Minor League Baseball Experience begins at the New Moon Tavern before the game. It begins in Fred Vranizan's long tunnel across the street from the stadium, Westside, the New Moon Tavern, where pennants hanging from the ceiling cite championship years for the Beavers, where the walls are papered with superstars from Ruth to Mays, where behind the bar autographed baseballs and Louisville sluggers are found instead of go-go girls. With luck the temperature is dropping below eighty outside, though still warm enough to draw brow-beads and to whet the thirst. And if you're thirsty the Baseball Experience begins an hour before batting lineups are exchanged at home plate, begins with a beer and a nod to Fred, the man with the gray handle-bar moustache. Slap down a quarter, get back a glass of beer, a dime and a pass good for half-price admission to the game. What happens next is up to you, baseball fans. If you want to have a quiet beer, Fred obliges. If you want to talk, and especially talk baseball, Fred's ready. Perhaps you have a question: "Say, when did DiMaggio go up anyway?" Fred refers the question to the guy two barstools down and before the head on your beer drops, the whole place is talking baseball. At the stadium the players warm up with fungoes, and at the New Moon Tavern the fans do the same.

The New Moon is long and narrow, with entrances both on Burnside and opposite, a tavern barely wide enough to stick an aisle between the booths and the bar. Into this tunnel are stuffed relics of baseball's history. The décor is not without its recognition of the hometown Beavers but the general atmosphere emphasizes baseball as game and tradition. Sitting in the close quarters of the New Moon Tavern is rather like being bound in a bubblegum wrapper with all two hundred baseball cards you saved as a kid. Breathe too heavily and overhead a 1906 championship pennant may flutter and tickle your bald spot.

To move across the street to the stadium is to become aware of how baseball has changed. But also of how it hasn't changed, despite rumors which would have modern baseball without traditional elements. If you happened to get Fred started at the New Moon, no doubt you heard that baseball went downhill with the expansion of the majors. In the "old days" even a losing team had its national star, as the Pirates had Ralph Kiner. Each team, before Brooklyn became Los Angeles and Boston became Milwaukee became—poof!—Atlanta, in the days of baseball stability each team had its regular lineup, a batting order of personalities who stayed around long enough to become known to the fans. Today a player must wear mod clothes or marry a Playmate of the Month to become a sports-page personality. In the "old days" every regular on the team, including reliefers and pinch hitters, was well-known to the hometown fans from prolonged exposure. What kind of exposure do the Beavers get when they lose their catcher by a long-distance phone call in the middle of a ballgame?

Moving to the ballpark, then, one is aware of a radical change. Out on the green carpet (not grass) you will find the hometown heroes, fans, but who can say how many will still be in town next season? A question to contemplate over a paper cup of beer. Don't think the atmosphere has changed because we've left the likes of DiMaggio and Musial on the walls of the New Moon to enter the minor leagues. It's not that. When I was a kid and an Angel fan, Chuck Conners and Steve Bilko were every bit as tall as Gil Hodges and Ted Williams. We speak now of the gods and had Ares changed his allegiance from War to Peace overnight, the Greeks would have become atheists.

But it's still too hot to compare superstars to gods. Beer and relaxation in the sun, a hot dog and peanuts for dinner—this is the direction our Baseball Experience takes. At home plate stands a man in blue, representing the Establishment, and baseball remains baseball because someone in the stands is booing.

A small crowd has turned out to welcome the Beavers home from a road trip—an embarrassingly small crowd, it must be admitted, of under a thousand. Die-hard Beaver fans? Not entirely, although the rooters audibly are present. Others are simply baseball fans out to see a game, any game, because baseball is baseball. At this juncture, if the reporter may indulge in lofty speculation, baseball ceases to be religion (as in gods and superstars and the worship of personalities, the baseball of the "old days") and becomes psychotherapy. To throw the change-up pitch: The Portland Urban Minor League Baseball Experience is a game, indeed, but it's a game in which the fans do most of the playing.

The therapeutic value of baseball is that it is slow. SLOW! This is significant. Why, baseball may be the last slow dance left in America! Consider the pitcher's delivery: for three or four seconds the pitcher contemplates the signal from the catcher, for a few more seconds his arms slowly begin the windup, then one leg lifts, the upper body leans back for leverage and comes forward again, the pitching arm whipping the ball to the plate, a sequence which takes another several seconds to complete. It takes the pitcher some ten seconds to throw the ball, which more often than not is taken by the batter for a ball or strike. This, baseball fans, is the most action you'll see in the next half-minute or more.

Which is baseball's advantage! Where else can one daydream for minutes on end and very likely miss none of the action? The answer, of course, is when watching television, which has become baseball's greatest rival. But the television set is at home, garrison also of the telephone. And telephones ring! Baseball, in contrast, provides unique relief from speedy technologyland. Baseball is a vacation close to home, a trout stream in the city, an inexpensive psychotherapy.

Only adult fans are stretched out on the analyst's couch, however. Kids do at the ballpark what they do everywhere else— they progressively sit still, wiggle, make faces, laugh, shout, scream, play tag, and wrestle. Adults do exactly the same, in a manner of speaking, but such carryings-on for them are quite out of workaday character. The ballpark permits what the office does not—leisure and playful antics. While all spectator sports allow something of the latter, baseball is unique in being performed at such a relaxing—at such a painstakingly slow!—pace. Throw away your watches when you venture out to support the Beavers because the baseball therapist can't tell time.

Why therapy? someone must be asking. The reply will be in cultural terms. Just as baseball is tranquilizing relief from the adult's busy world of making (to use a moot term) "a living," and is special relief in contemporary leagues where there are few known personalities to elicit the prolonged worshipping instincts, so also is baseball a game played BY THE FANS, a game which lets the fans relieve cultural frustrations in culturally harmless ways. The New Moon Tavern is a cathedral but the ballpark is something closer to a convention hall for New Politics. Baseball fans are the loudest radicals in Portland. They are notorious for being anti-Establishment, which is to say they prefer self-righteous anarchy to the lawful order of the umpire. There must be a strong rebellious trait in the American character, for by the fifth inning adult fans who gave earlier innings only listless attention—such fun to daydream!—suddenly get to their feet to yell, "Throw the bum out!" Oh, it's great fun!

What is ironic is that the Baseball Experience, being space-bound, is not translated into cultural terms outside the ballpark. In fact, a father who last night thumbed an umpire today will reprimand his son for delivering a similar salutation to a college president. And therein lies the therapeutic aspect of baseball: baseball as dream, as wish fulfillment. The umpire is everyman's boss and booing him wins a promotion. Of course, this gets acted out only within the space-bound ballpark, for beyond the bleachers very different games are played. Once outside the stadium the fan is back in…the Real World (it's been called).

But for a few hours we can watch baseball on a warm night in Portland. We wear masks, we dance, we relax and wait for the umpire to elicit our disfavor, at which time we cry out for justice; we play out the festival that has made baseball America's most traditional and popular sport. We wage fun and war together, and may the umpire help the Tucson fan who takes a seat behind the Beaver dugout. Through the evening we sip beer or pop, we chew peanuts and hotdogs, we rid our lungs of urban contamination, and between innings we send the kids racing off with their winning ticket stubs to collect prizes. It's baseball! And if that last curve dropped low and inside—we saw it ourselves from behind third base—then let's let the umpire know it, fans, let him hear it! We shall overcome!

Yes, baseball fans, up on our feet to COMPLAIN! Why we're every bit as rebellious as Che Guevera and don't have to pay the social consequences. Baseball is our dance, the last slow dance in America. The Portland Urban Minor League Baseball Experience is a grand ol' game for warm nights in the grand ol' Pacific Northwest. LET'S HEAR IT, FANS! PLAY BALL!!

A good rhubarb deserves a relaxed last inning, agreed? The New Moon Tavern is the place to go before the game because it's a gallery of baseball and sets the mood. After the game, however, the baseball fan may prefer to go where many of the ballplayers themselves go, to The Bullpen Tavern, which is eastside across from the stadium. Behind the bar is John Hunt, a young man in Bermudas who might have belonged to a fraternity in school and played some ball himself. John's very cordial and knows enough baseball to have his own radio sports show.

We talk about the game for a moment and then decide it's time to come down. Beside the jukebox a pretty blonde in a miniskirt is fluttering with more appeal than a 1906 championship pennant. The New Moon's clientele is largely middle-aged and over, but here the crowd is collegiate and athletic. The Bullpen swings and the fact that players come here suggests a thesis: today a young first baseman would rather goggle at a pretty blonde than at an autographed picture of Lou Gehrig. So much for the "good old days."

Our Portland Beavers lost again, fans, but they'll be back tomorrow and will win, we keep the faith that they'll win. Some of us will be back to support them. A new game! But meanwhile, well, how about drawing another mug, John? The atmosphere is not exactly pure baseball at The Bullpen but the place swings, a pretty blonde is swaying by the jukebox, and there's nothing outside but—the Real World (it's been called).

7.13.69

five:

History & Nostalgia

159

"Timber's Comstock Lode" by Ellis Lucia
*"The West was never wilder than here. Knifings
and head bashings were a common occurrence.
The radical Wobblies kept things churning."*

"A Visit to the Barber" by Gerry Pratt
*"There was a smell about the barbershop in those days,
whiskey maybe, and the hard hair tonic they used to rub
into the bristles left standing across the top of your skull."*

"Homage to Vacant Lots" by Rick Rubin
*"After the cutters were through it seemed so shorn and yellow,
already dying under the sun, so flat and civilized, and though
we relished the sweet odor of cut grass, and realized that those
particular rules are made for the common good, we regretted
the passing of all that undisciplined greenness."*

TIMBER'S COMSTOCK LODE

Ellis Lucia

If you wanted action, it wasn't hard to find along the Grays Harbor waterfront. A man took his life in his hands by traveling alone. There were innumerable deadfalls where a logger or seaman might wind up with a knot on his head, his pocketbook considerably lighter, or take a breathless plunge through a trap door, leading to a lengthy sea voyage.

The skid road of this free-wheeling Washington seaport, in the roaring times of yesteryear, was among the world's wickedest, likened to San Francisco's Barbary Coast. Violence was a way of life. Yet even the tough proprietors of Aberdeen's many dives were visibly shaken one winter when the bodies of lumberjacks by the dozens began bobbing up amid the log booms. Someone was doing them in, and making a messy job of it. A Private Eye was hired to solve the mystery, which proved to be a Perry Mason thriller.

The bustling towns of Aberdeen and Hoquiam are still highballing lumber centers. Although calmer now, there remains a certain lustiness in the air. The old skid road has been wiped out by urban renewal, but not the rugged tradition, for big things happened here. The cattlemen had Dodge City; the lumbermen had The Harbor.

I like to think of it as timber's Comstock Lode. The Nevada Comstock, in case you aren't up on your Western history, was the greatest silver strike of all time. It spawned the Silver Kings, poured wealth into San Francisco, and helped finance the Civil War. In similar fashion, Grays Harbor was the epitome of old-time lumbering on the North American continent. There has been nothing like it since.

Around The Harbor, everything was perfect for mining the green gold—the time, the place, the natural conditions, the supply. Most of all the supply. There was more whopping big stuff in the surrounding hills than a logger might dream about. Like walking barefoot through clover.

"The noblest growth of fir, spruce, cedar and hemlock ever found in the civilized world," declared one early observer.

This timber Eldorado was astounding. The virgin trees, hundreds of years old, were thick as blades of grass. The forests ran three to four million board feet to the forty, some 50 billion board feet in all. The mighty trees measured over five feet in diameter and 180 feet sawlog length to the first branches. It was a rich lode, for the take was 30 billion board feet in 50 years. And the lumbermen became millionaires.

There is an intriguing legend about one particular tract, north of Hoquiam. It was Old 21-9, branded by loggers as the "Mother Township" of the Douglas fir region. The trees were of such grand magnificence, two billion board feet in 28 sections, that the lumberjacks believed from this place spread all the great Douglas fir forests of the Pacific Northwest.

Over 12,000 men in tin pants and caulked boots worked in the bayfront's 37 screaming sawmills, in numerous allied industries, and in the back country during the boom times of the first three decades of this century. Specialty plants turned out 7,250 doors daily, shingles, lath, box shook, molding, finished cabinet pieces and fine piano sounding boards of coveted Sitka spruce stock. Some of the world's biggest logging and lumbering equipment was manufactured by local machine shops. Ten great logging companies, employing thousands, and numerous small outfits got out the timber. Another big outfit handled the log drives. There were 20 railroads hauling out the hefty logs. Aberdeen, after a hard struggle, also got its own branch to the mainline, built of salvaged rails from a shipwreck near the mouth of the bay. Folks knew when they were nearing town from the strange music played by the wheels on the pocked rails.

That broad bay was a mad scramble of sailing vessels and steam schooners. In a single year, 880 ships called to gulp down quantities of lumber for ports of the world, while 17,905 freight cars hauled off the balance of the year's cut of 1½ billion board feet. During the six climactic years, 1924–29, the annual output averaged 1,352,000,000 board feet. Yet in the midst of this frantic harvest, rugged lumberjacks of the Polson Brothers logging outfit, one of biggest of all time, were setting out tiny seedlings in cutover lands. At Grays Harbor the lumbermen came full circle, beginning to get religion. It was here that the first tree farms were born, a concept that has since spread across the nation.

Sawmills had been humming around Puget Sound and in Oregon for decades before lumbermen discovered this Big Bonanza. In 1881, Charles Stevens and William Anderson operated a small mill on the Chehalis River. That same summer Captain A.M. Simpson, an expert at falling trees, sent an aide north for a look. George Emerson staked a claim and returned to California in pent-up excitement. Next year they were back with sawmill gear and soon shipped out the first boards.

Colorful Captain Simpson was truly the father of Aberdeen. He was a lumberman of the first order, with mills strung all along the coast and later an estate at Coos Bay, now Shore Acres state park. He was immortalized in a unique way. Among his workers was Peter B. Kyne, who kept the books. Kyne had a way with words as well as figures. From his boss he fashioned the redoubtable Cappy Ricks, one of the most memorable characters of American magazine and book fiction of the time. Kyne, who later moved to San Francisco, also drew many incidents for his novels from The Harbor.

The surrounding hills were slotted with streams, swelled by heavy rainfalls much of the year. A special system was devised for getting the great logs to the bay. "Splash dams" in series of up to eight were built on the streams. When the deluge came, the dams were opened and the unleashed logs lunged downstream in some of the maddest drives on record.

"Splash" became part of the Harbor's lingo, long before there were astronauts. It was what they called the Fourth of July celebration, the West's first great logging show. Then thousands of loggers came to town, like trail-weary cowpokes, after six months in the brush. When the wild blow-in was over, the towns awoke with massive hangovers, striving to get things on an even keel again.

There were log pirates on the bay and thieves along lawless skid road. Shanghaiing was a common practice, to fill out the ship crews. There were spectacular mill and forest fires, railroad wrecks, street fights, saloon and bagnio brawls, strikes and riots. The West was never wilder than here. Knifings and head bashings were a common occurrence. The radical Wobblies kept things churning. Lonely men came, worked awhile, and went away, some forever. When the mill changed shifts, the roar of heavy boots was like a cattle stampede on "Plank Island," as Aberdeen was called.

Proprietors of the dives grew rich on the mill hands and the loggers. Dollars rolled into the barkeeps' pockets and the stockings of the girls of celebrated Hume Street's line. The city got its share, too. Aberdeen collected $1,000 a year for a saloon license, and there were 50 of them. The Palm Dance hall was the most notorious, with five barkeeps, four bouncers and 40 girls. On opening night, there was a mighty brawl and a man was killed, scalped they said by a spiked scantling swung wildly through the air. But even that adverse publicity didn't keep The Palm from long being a favorite play center.

Far back in the hills Big John Turnow terrorized loggers and ranchers by swinging through the trees like Tarzan and shooting those who tried to bring him in. At last, the Wild Man of the Olympics was killed by a brave deputy sheriff and everyone breathed easier.

Aberdeen, meanwhile, had its own troubles, being branded "The Port of Missing Men." Many loggers and sailors were transients. When they didn't report nobody thought much of it. Then those stark forms, with crushed skulls and bullets through the heart, began showing up in the bay. By winter's end, 43 had been fished out. It struck terror in the hearts of even the toughest lumberjacks.

The long trail led to Billy Gohl, personable agent of the Sailors Union. Gohl was everybody's friend, so it seemed. He operated from an office above the Grand Saloon, and would hold a fellow's pay while he prowled the Hume Street joints. But not everybody liked Billy. For one thing he had the bold audacity to paint the outhouse, hanging over the end of the pier behind his place, a bright vermilion. On a certain afternoon Skipper Michael McCaroon was heading his vessel downstream. He couldn't resist, and swung the ship so the jib boom neatly clipped that gaudy outhouse. Off she went, with the two holer swinging from the boomstick. Too bad, thought McCaroon, that Billy wasn't inside.

Unknown to most, Gohl had a background of Skagway, where the infamous Soapy Smith operated. He was quietly eliminating trusting loggers and mariners whose back pay he held. Then he'd haul the remains out to sea. But Gohl grew lazy and began dumping his victims in the bay and rivers. That proved his downfall. Now many things came into focus. Besides, with such a name, how could it be otherwise?

The trial was a sensation; editions of the local paper sold out within moments after hitting the street. The newsboys never had it so good. It seemed that Billy had operated his chamber of horrors for years and was responsible for 140 deaths, possibly a hundred others. It was by far the greatest mass murder on record. The Mad Monster of Aberdeen, as he was called, was sent to the state penitentiary at Walla Walla, later being transferred to the insane asylum where he lived for 20 years.

Suspicions about the extent of Gohl's activities were confirmed even further. When workmen were laying new water and sewer lines along the Aberdeen waterfront years later, they dug into areas filled with human bones. These were believed to be "more of Gohl's catacombs."

The good citizens of the community labored long to improve Aberdeen's image. A milestone was achieved when Hume Street was changed to State Street. But the greatest day came in 1927, just 40 years ago, when Lindbergh flew the Atlantic. The Harbor flew right along with him. Later, on his national tour, Lindy dipped the wing of his plane over the rowdy areas where her super-structure was manufactured. That was a mighty proud moment for timber's Comstock Lode.

4.2.67

A VISIT TO THE BARBER

Gerry Pratt

On the late television commercials they are selling do-it-yourself hair cutting kits. Poppa is in the chair and his wife is zipping this thing up his neck just like it's induction day all over again. As his ears begin appearing and his wife is smiling into the cameras, a pitchman begins explaining how you can make enough money for a vacation trip to Europe just by cutting your own hair.

He's not kidding. The price of haircuts has been going up faster than oil producers' bank balances. I am of this century, and I can remember haircuts at two bits a clip, and I can remember barbers who thought a razor cut was something you tried to patch over with toilet paper.

No more. Even that old saw, "Shave and a haircut, six bits," seems to have been something out of the 18th Century. I mean, haircuts today are four dollars apiece, with an appointment, and if you don't leave the barber a half or more, chances are you are a long time between appointments. Some guys are even turning to beauty parlors, and there it is a matter of hair styling and you never know what that's going to cost.

Why so agitated? Well, it's great to have the barber make a buck. But it has just been suggested to my heir apparent that he see about getting his biblical hairstyle shortened to conform with the job market. This kid says he would, but he can't afford it. The only kids who are getting haircuts these days are the ones going through the recruiting centers. The haircut is one of the military fringe benefits that has meaning.

What we need in this era of nostalgia is a return to the real barbershop, like the one we had on Yew Street in a store front. The barber there was a World War II Irish Fuselier who learned his trade in His Majesty's Service. He was gray and brutal with the clippers when I knew him, tired around the shoulders so his arms would drop to his sides and he would let out a burst of air with every series of passes at your head. It was exhausting work, and looking back you can see now that his feet must have resented the job terribly. You could tell the way he laid down his newspaper and looked up at you when you came through the door. There was a small bell over the door in case he was in the toilet in the back of the shop and he was there a lot in the late years when he cut hair with a glassy-eyed stare and made wild, reckless passes with the clippers.

Those were not the electric clippers you kids know about today. They were squeeze clippers, and this old barber would hook his arthritic fingers around the handles and squeeze, clip, clip. Sometimes when he was tired, he would pull the clippers away half way through the squeeze and the hair would come out by the roots. "Oops. Gotcha that time," and he would wipe the back of his hand across his nose in a gesture of apology.

There was a smell about the barbershop in those days, whiskey maybe, and the hard hair tonic they used to rub into the bristles left standing across the top of your skull. That was a strange, powerful tonic, mostly water but enough of some secret military potion mixed in to make it sit up like cement so that when the barber combed your hair, the bristles popping up on either side above the ears, it was as if the part had been sliced in stone and neither wind nor rain would ease the part for a week or more.

"Good morning," said the barber, as if it was really your idea and he was not committed to it at all. He tucked the paper into the back of his chair and pushed himself to his feet. There was pain in the way he would reach for the soiled sheet that hung over the back of the barber chair.

"Shave? Or just a haircut?" And he would laugh at that and pinch your cheeks between his fingers. "No. That's just bum fuzz, lad. But wait a while; shaving is a blessing that comes later."

And he would slap the board across the arms of the barber chair and stand back while you climbed into the perch. It was then you handed him the quarter. With that he began, starting low on the nape of your neck beneath the line where the sheet tucked into your shirt so that the small clippings dropped down your back and drew your shoulder blades into a tense twitch. "Easy now. Sit still. That pull a little? Well, sit still or we are going to lose an ear."

There was no question about style. You got into the chair and he turned you away from the mirror and left you facing the door until he was finished, right to the point where he whipped the lather from his shaving mug and scraped the straight razor down your neck. "Clean at the back the way your mother wants it," he would say.

Then with a flourish he would spin the chair, whip away the sheet so the hair clippings flew up into your face and ask with sudden authority in his voice, "That's better, eh?"

And for an instant, summer or winter, you would look into the face of a stranger, a thin boy with oh, such large protruding ears. And the barber then would thumb press to your head those hairs that stood up in defiance of his secret tonic and push you out of the chair. And the outside air struck cool and fresh to the naked sides of your head.

You took the haircut home so Momma could see if you got your money's worth. She always seemed a little hurt when you came home from the barbershop. It was as if you had grown a little while you had been away, and after she looked it over and told you it looked nice, you knew somewhere inside that indeed you had. And all for a quarter.

9.21.75

171

HOMAGE TO VACANT LOTS

Rick Rubin

Down the street and around the corner there was a vacant lot that had not yet been mowed. We discovered it on an evening stroll.

Each vacant lot has its own personality, of course, mostly created by the type of vegetation it supports. This one was entirely covered with that tall sort of grass, four or more feet high, that has a feathery head somewhat like wheat. It sways and bends in any breeze, and eventually sags over of its own weight in a graceful curve.

Not all uncut vacant lots are attractive, but this one had great charm. Walking by on the sidewalk one felt as though one were some swift and narrow ship, a destroyer perhaps or large private yacht, plowing through a billowing sea. The sidewalk registered only as a sort of depression between the grass of the lot and the grass of the equally overgrown parking strip. We plowed through, then turned around and did it again feeling and hearing the tall dry grass whisper against our clothing.

However, the other side of the vacant lot situation was represented by the former lawn of a nearby old house, no longer occupied, where blackberries had taken over. Walking by that shaggy place we felt the blackberry vines like malignant octopus tentacles, reaching out to snag and rip and tear, perhaps to devour.

Between the two extremes of pure grass and pure blackberries there are a hundred variations. A block or two further on the same street there was an overgrown sidewalk along the edge of the state's border strip above a freeway. Here the blackberries were small and inoffensive, but beginning to bear their small sweet fruit, and sweet peas were blossoming out across the concrete and up on the state wire fence. There was vetch, blooming purple, and the beginnings of small maple and horse chestnut trees, plus grass of the various kinds, the wheat-like one described before, and the kind with a narrow, hard green stem topped by a mealy little cylinder that eventually extrudes little yellow dots of pollen and seeds.

We spotted thistle too, and the inevitable morning glories and ivy and other climbing or trailing plants. It makes one ashamed of not knowing the names of all the plants one lives with daily like next-door neighbors, yet if one has lived here long enough their identities are well known, if not their official titles. There was one weed, I think we called it snake grass when I was a boy, a watery, jointed growth with green whiskers all around at every jointed level, found anywhere that it is wet or even moist. What its real name is I can't even guess.

The particular cause of our delight with the uncut vacant lots was that a few days before the owner of the vacant lots on either side of the house we live in had sent around a crew to cut down the vegetation. We had been watching those lots with delight, the battle between the blackberries and the grass and the vetch for room to live, the undulating greenness of the lots under any wind. After the cutters were through it seemed so shorn and yellow, already dying under the sun, so flat and civilized, and though we relished the sweet odor of cut grass, and realized that those particular rules are made for the common good, we regretted the passing of all that undisciplined greenness.

Out of curiosity, not being landowners ourselves, we called the city to find out exactly what the rules are on vacant lots. We were connected with the Bureau of Nuisance Abatement of the Department of Public Affairs. We were informed that it is mostly on account of fire hazards that vacant lots must be cut before the grass dries in the spring, and kept cut from April through September, but, he suggested, aesthetics too have their place in the regulation.

We let the aesthetics part go; arguments over the telephone

are likely to be tedious and difficult. The lot and one-half of the adjacent street area, should the street be unimproved, must be shorn of all grass, ferns, weeds and other noxious vegetation, plus any dead trees, by the landholder. We wondered who had defined ferns as noxious vegetation, but let it go. The vegetation, we learned, must be kept under ten inches.

If the property owner doesn't shear the lot of his own accord the city sends out a crew. They inspect the city's vacant lots beginning the first of May, and check again in June to see that the order has been complied with. Last year they sent out 3,000 notices, and spend something like $25,000 contracting out the work of cutting 1,000 to 1,200 vacant lots, the work done privately and billed by the city to the owner. Of course complaints called in during the summer will also be acted upon.

Still, when next we looked, those vacant lots down the street and around the corner were still bravely resisting urban neatness, and at least a few of them must belong to city or state or federal government, the ones by the edge of the freeway fence, so the matter does not seem one of great urgency.

Another reason we enjoyed those uncut lots so well, beyond the anarchistic and the aesthetic, was a memory of boyhood. Girls do not seem to have too much affinity for vacant lots, but for boys life would not be the same without at least one vacant lot nearby, unless of course there is an actual forest. It is almost as important as the need for a haunted house to test one's courage against.

We played games of ball and tag on our vacant lot, and more structured games like Red Rover Come Over. Kick the can, however, was always played in the street, probably for the more satisfactory noise it made. In vacant lots we built forts, and discovered or created secret paths through the blackberries to even more secret green-walled rooms, where we could divulge or keep enormous secrets and perhaps even a treasure or two.

Now-a-days there seem to be fewer vacant lots available where most of the kids live. Suburban tracts are not laid out in favor of vacant areas; each lot must have its house. Eventually some of those houses will grow old and be pulled down no doubt, but as yet and for a considerable time to come they are still standing. The older neighborhoods, not so far out, are fuller now than they used to be. The empty lots have given way to progress and the growth of population. Only in older still-transitional neighborhoods like our own, where business offices and light industry are moving and people moving out, where old houses are being pulled down and not immediately replaced, does the vacant lot density seem to be increasing, and that is only a phase. We can see progress marching inexorably toward us.

One is probably incorrect to think that Portland has now, or ever did have, more vacant lots than elsewhere. But surely there are few places on earth where the lots grow up so high and thick and lush so naturally, where unattended places return so quickly to wilderness. Not just Portland, really, more properly the entire Pacific Northwest rain strip. Oregon, Washington and British Columbia, where everything grows so well. If one is a Northwesterner living in San Francisco or New York, the vacant lots of home loom large in one's memory.

By the time you read this, no doubt, the cutters will have been around for those lots down around the corner, and we will have to wait until May or June of next year to walk a sidewalk like a ship through a sea of grass. That, or go out into the country, to a field, and do it there. But it is not quite the same in the country, for one is not walking on the concrete sidewalk, nor savoring how the grass and undergrowth, given a few months leeway, cover the hard and rectilinear signs of what men choose to call progress.

5.7.67

EXCERPTS FROM NOTEWORTHY STORIES

So Long, Woody: Woody Guthrie in the Northwest
by Ralph Friedman
5.8.66

"One thing for sure: among the dust bowl Okies, who were his soul kin, he was as much at home as turnips to greens. There was hardly a soul in those ditch weed camps who was second cousin to a dollar, so Woody settled for what the other Okies were eating, and maybe a pair of patched pants or a sweater two sizes too big or a couple of nickels to carry him on his way. Every once in a while our drifting paths would cross, like the smoke of two twig fires sieving through each other.

"Just before I entered the Army I heard Woody singing with The Weavers, the other fellows being Pete Seeger, Lee Hays and Millard Lampell, certainly the most gifted quartet of all folk singers. They were rousing out some of Woody's songs, with him staying mostly in the background, maybe just half a step behind the others, as was his way. A lot of young singers, on their way to the bank, could take a few lessons in humility from the way Woody performed."

Requiem for a Barn
by Carl Gohs
5.19.68

"Tom O'Donnell's barn is down and gone; no matter, it was useless long since—a tree having neither leaves nor fruit and so dead. The barn stood with several Victorian cottages on a half block at NW 19th and Thurman. Tom is now dead six months and the barn is gone and the spot where it stood is wiped clean.

"...So it is elsewhere in the city, and regrettably, it possibly is right that much of it should go—the old barns, old houses, great trees, remnants of orchards. It's just that it's sad to see ALL of them go."

There Were Black Pioneers, Too
by Roger Tetlow
10.5.69

"Long before Oregon became a state, two men entered the Oregon country in different ways and from different directions. James D. Saules came by sea, tumbling in over the Columbia River bar in the wreck of the Peacock in 1841. Winslow Anderson arrived from California by horseback as a member of the famed Ewing Young party in 1834. Each of these two men followed an equally exciting life until they met on the Clackamas prairie in 1843, took part in one of the most significant events in Oregon history, and then parted, each following a different path to obscurity and death.

"Both James D. Saules and Winslow Anderson were black men."

The Way to Wounded Knee
by Art Raymond
4.15.73

"American Indian spokesmen, both great and small, have pleaded for action, for results. Talk, talk, talk and the words sound good. The words have sounded good from the BIA (Bureau of Indian Affairs) from the time of President Jackson to this day. But the talk and the words have not brought the Indian peoples out of the economic doldrums nor the social servitude in which they exist.

"That is why in February, 1973, members of the Indian Movement (AIM) occupied Wounded Knee. Settled in the large rolling foothills of the sacred Black Hills of the Sioux, Wounded Knee is in itself a symbol of the Sioux. Its big hills, and sweeping valleys, marked by tree- and brush-lined streams, stand as a symbol of the Sioux for all time.

"Regardless of the eventual outcome, Wounded Knee will not be brushed aside or forgotten. It will stand forever as a symbol of man's inhumanity to man."

Translation: The Indian's Dilemma
by Barry Lopez
7.29.73

"The Indian's world view is generally circular. He sees his life as already complete at each moment. There is, therefore, no need to 'progress'; rather, he expands as he grows older, like a ballooning sphere. The past and the present, not the future, are important to him. He has a strong sense of balance and harmony with the physical world and tends to live by negotiating with his environment. He is an opportunist, not a planner. He does not regard the earth as a hostile place and makes no long range plans to control it."

A Boy and His Mitt
by Steve Erickson
9.7.75

"The mitt, the mitt. It is really a glove, but he'll call it a mitt to his grave.

"It is a Wilson Ball Hawk, manufactured only briefly before the company desisted in embarrassment. The two-fingered model confounds even its occasional admirers. On the little finger, which is bigger than the thumb, are the faded instructions, 'two fingers here.'

"The mitt used to have padding, but en route to the major leagues its owner removed it. Deeper pocket. This accentuated the pain from catching line drives, but big-leaguers, he believed then, don't cry.

"It is, incidentally, a righthanded mitt with a southpaw personality. On its wristband the boy emblazoned his initials with a woodburning set."

The Day Vanport Died
by Lynda Lesowski
5.21.78

"Today Vanport is West Delta Park, a grassy expanse intersected by little-traveled N. Broadacre and N. Force Avenues;

people go there to jog, hurl Frisbees and play soccer. It's hard to imagine 800 apartment buildings imposed on this bucolic scene. In its heyday Vanport had 179 service buildings, three grade schools, four shopping centers, two administration buildings, recreation centers, a post office, a hospital, a fire department, churches, sheriff's office, jail, a newspaper and Vanport College, which was set up to meet post-war overcrowding at state schools. There were 17½ miles of paved roads and 44 miles of pathways. It was a vital, modern community, even though considered just a temporary stop by those who lived there, and the people of Vanport lived together and worked for the improvement of their town in a community spirit rarely seen today."

(Note: At 4:05 p.m. on May 30, 1948, a dike holding back the Columbia River gave way, flooding and destroying the community of Vanport. Fifteen people died.)

six:

The Arts

"Opera in Portland: Coming On Fortissimo"
by Charles Gould
"In 1957, the Civic Opera was reorganized. By ordinance, the City of Portland authorized support for the Theatre Arts Opera Association through the Recreation Division of the Bureau of Parks and Public Recreation."

"Eugene's Very Little Theater"
by Dorothy Velasco
"The company is unique in that it has continuously functioned for 50 seasons, has always been self-supporting, and operates out of its very own theater building. It is doubtful that any other community theater in the country can duplicate all those claims."

OPERA IN PORTLAND:
COMING ON FORTISSIMO

Charles Gould

The first operatic production in the Pacific Northwest took place in midsummer, 1867, in Portland's Oro Fino Theatre. The Oro Fino was a two-story wooden-frame building with a downstairs saloon and an upstairs hall large enough to handle most entertainments likely to wander out of the wilderness at that time, such as the light-traveling variety and minstrel troupes with the usual complement of four performers.

The Bianchi Opera Company arrived by steamer from San Francisco with a full force of personnel—five singers and a pianist. The reigning star of the company, Signora Bianchi (called "The Mother of San Francisco Opera") stayed at home. Nevertheless, her equally gifted husband, Signor Bianchi, the company's founder, was on hand to undertake all the tenor roles in all performances. Signorina Bellini, Signora Bianchi's replacement, was to do all the lead soprano parts, and, according to *The Oregonian*, she "has been spoken of by the music critics of San Francisco as a charming prima donna and an accomplished artiste."

The company performed seven evenings in Portland with intermittent one-night stands in Vancouver, Oregon City and Salem. All of their performances, with the exception of scenery and choruses, were given in their entirety, in operatic costume, to piano accompaniment. They began their season with "Il Trovatore" and ended with "La Traviata." Portland performances also included "Norma," "Lucia di Lammermoor," "La Somnambula" and, in one evening, "Lucrezia Borgia," "Ernani" and Signor Bianchi's rendition of Arditi's then-famous vocal waltz, "Il Bacio"—the kiss. All performances met with small but enthusiastic audiences and the company did not realize the monetary returns expected. Though the company continued to travel to secluded Western communities, it never returned to Portland.

Not only was the Bianchi Opera Company the vanguard of opera in the Northwest, it also opened "an era in the history of dramatic entertainments in Portland," wrote *The Oregonian* at the time.

In the next two decades, a few more intrepid opera companies found their way into Oregon, though by this time travel had been eased considerably by newly constructed railroad lines. These post-Bianchi performers were sure to find the New Market Theatre's accommodations a vast improvement over the Oro Fino's hall above the saloon.

The New Market, a joint enterprise of Capt. A. P. Ankeny and Andrew J. Watson, was built "entirely of bricks and iron." It was opened to the public in 1875 with a seating capacity of 1,200. Because of its size and elegance, the larger traveling shows put Portland and the New Market on their itinerary. The New Market can still be seen today on Ankeny Street between SW First and Second avenues. The century-old structure is a parking facility.

In 1890, the Marquam Grand Opera House opened its doors. "At last," proclaimed a contemporary newspaper, "the event which has stood out so prominently before the amusement public for weeks past, the inauguration of an opera house which can be the pride of every citizen of Portland, is close at hand. Tomorrow night will see the dedication of this structure and by an organization that stands at the head of all musical attractions in the country."

The Emma Juch Grand Opera Company opened the Marquam Grand's first week of entertainment with Gounod's "Faust." "Miss Juch is everywhere regarded," wrote *The Oregonian*, "as the ideal Marguerite, and she has, perhaps, received more unqualified praise from her rendering of that role than was ever bestowed before upon an American artiste."

In keeping with the grandeur of the event, the Marquam's program cautioned its patrons: "Catcalls, whistling and stamping feet positively prohibited."

Emma Juch, though at that time just 24 years old, was already a diva of considerable experience, talent and stamina. She sang the principal role in six different operas on six consecutive evenings; she returned a year later and repeated this formidable undertaking in an equal number of dissimilar roles.

Although few opera companies the caliber of the Emma Juch Grand Opera Company found their way to Portland before the turn of the century, the city was rarely without this form of entertainment. Throughout the 1880s, English versions of popular European comic operas and operettas were held nightly in a number of "opera" houses in the city. Particular favorites with Portland audiences were operettas by Offenbach, Lecocq, Planquette, Audran, Von Suppe, Strauss, Gilbert and Sullivan, and John Philip Sousa. Works by these and other composers were presented by resident companies at the New Park, Casino and Tivoli. The New Market and, a little later, the Marquam Grand occasionally hosted local and touring opera companies.

The Tivoli and Casino had sizable repertoires which permitted them to change programs weekly. The Tivoli had the following announcement published in the *Portland Daily News* in 1884: "The management of the Tivoli yesterday decided to close up for a few days, to allow the members of the company to take a much-needed rest. The company has played for over three months without missing a night, and a short rest will do them some good. On Saturday the house will be reopened with 'Olivette.' As soon as practicable a new opera will be rehearsed."

The floors of these small "opera" houses were covered with sawdust and the customers sat at tables. Before performances and during intermission, white-aproned waiters meandered through the crowd hawking "Drinks and Cigars!" Performances took place in the smoke–filled room. In a letter to *The Oregonian*, one of the Casino's patrons had this recollection: "Notwithstanding all of the roughness of the place, it was patronized by the best people. The women did not smoke, but many of them did drink to some extent...The gallery was for hoodlums. I use the word in its fullest meaning. The galleries of the theaters at that time were rough and noisy places, but they were the criterion of the show. If the gallery was pleased, the show was a success...It was necessary to have a policeman in attendance to preserve order. No woman ever sat in the gallery."

Portlanders had many opportunities to see and hear the greatest singers of their day in local recitals—David Bispham, Emilio de Gogorza, Leo Slezak, Titta Ruffo, Adelina Patti, Emma Calve, Nellie Melba, Johanna Gadski. Particular Portland favorites and frequent visitors were Lillian Nordica and Ernestine Schumann-Heink.

Portland's most exciting operatic year was in 1913. A special train from San Francisco was heralded along its way through Oregon. It arrived in Portland carrying the Chicago Opera Company—sets, costume, stagehands, managerial personnel, 85 musicians, a chorus of 75 and a distinguished group of soloists headed by Mary Garden and Luisa Tetrazzini. In all, about 200 people.

During its short stay the opera was front-page news. There was so much excitement in the air that even hyperbole became common: "Half of Portland," wrote *The Oregonian*, "stood banked on the street and sidewalks in front of the Orpheum last night and watched the other half passing in through the lobby to witness the opening performance of the Chicago Grand Opera Company." Actually, the opening night crowd was only half the attendance that greeted the two subsequent performances featuring Mary Garden and Luisa Tetrazzini. Nevertheless, the turnout was considerable and society was in its glory. Yards of newspaper columns were devoted to the ladies and their attire—"ermine," "sable," "priceless jewels." *The Oregonian* observed that "the head ornaments were in large measure confined to bands of diamond or pearls, holding flowing aigrettes, osprey or tiny plumes. Portland has never before seen such a collection of magnificent jewels at any one function." *The Evening Telegram* summed up what all the newspapers were spending thousands of words on: "There have been festal occasions, brilliant social functions, matchless entertainments of various kinds that have elicited the support and presence of the flower and chivalry of the city, but the Chicago Grand Opera Company makes every comparison of what has gone before seem sacrilege, and many a day is likely to come and go ere Portland sees its like again."

All this excitement and the company only stayed three days to perform four complete operas and the second act of Offenbach's "The Tales of Hoffmann." "Hoffmann," sung in French, was the second half of a matinee featuring Engelbert Humperdinck's relatively short "Hansel and Gretel." The bulk of the company's critical acclaim was evenly distributed between Mary Garden, for her "Thaïs," and Luisa Tetrazzini, for her "Lucia." Incidentally, the visiting Chicago Opera orchestra had ten more members than the local symphony had at that time. The Chicago Opera returned to Portland five more times (the last time in 1931).

Portland had its own outstanding opera company in 1917; it bore the same name as the present company—Portland Opera Association. Its organizer was a remarkable Italian of vast operatic experience, Roberto Corruccini. He had been affiliated with the Hammerstein Grand Opera Company of New York and the Melba Grand Opera Company of Australia before settling in Portland. As musical director and conductor of the local company, Corruccini brought before Portland audiences operas the city had never before seen and some, like Otto Nicolai's "Merry Wives of Windsor," that have not been produced here since. In those days, ticket prices ran from 50 cents to $1.50; today, the low ticket is $5 and the high $22. Roberto Corruccini continually presented meritorious operatic productions using local singers and musicians. He alone was the vital force of the company. Upon his death in 1923, the Portland Opera Association also expired.

Touring companies continued to play Portland. The San Carlo Opera Company appeared almost annually from 1918 to 1948 to perform a one-week season of eight operas. The San Carlo rarely boasted outstanding artists, but performances were uniformly good and the admission price was always reasonable. It was said of its manager, Fortune Gallo, that he was the only man in the country who could make money producing opera.

Throughout its musical history, Portland has attempted, with varying degrees of success, to build its own first-rate opera company. The present company, the Portland Opera Association, now ten years old, actually began 24 years ago with a summer production of Verdi's "Aïda" in Washington Park by the newly formed Portland Civic Opera Association. The 1950 "Aïda" was the cooperative venture of the Musicians' Union Local 99 (Herman Kenin, president), the Portland Park Recreation Bureau (Dorothea Lensch, director) and the Portland School of Music (Ariel Rubstein, director). As the program note stated, "All members of the cast, production and promotion have generously given of their time, money and talent so that these performances of the opera AÏDA may be presented FREE to the people of Portland."

"Aïda" was a 100-percent local production, with 52 musicians conducted by Rubstein. Featured were nine soloists, a chorus of 60, 18 dancers and one camel driver. The Washington Park opera was a highly successful endeavor that resulted the next year in the incorporation of the Portland Civic Opera Association, which continued for seven years under the conductorship of Ariel Rubstein and, later, Eugene Fuerst.

In 1957, the Civic Opera was reorganized. By ordinance, the City of Portland authorized support for the Theatre Arts Opera Association through the Recreation Division of the Bureau of Parks and Public Recreation. Fuerst continued as the general director and conductor of the new company. Most of the performances of the Portland Civic Theatre Arts Opera companies were given in high school auditoriums and the Oriental Theatre. The Theatre Arts group continued until 1964, when it was reorganized and incorporated as the present company, the Portland Opera Association.

In its first decade of operation, the Portland Opera Association has presented over 100 performances. Since 1968, the renovated Portland Civic Auditorium has been the POA's permanent home. Free Washington Park operatic concerts are still held each summer.

From the POA's founding in 1964 until 1966, its general director and conductor was Henry Holt. Prior to his Portland appointment, Holt was associated with the Opera House of Coblenz, Germany. Holt is presently music and educational director of the Seattle Opera Association. The baton of the POA was passed to Herbert Weiskopf.

Weiskopf, with a broad European musical background, came to the United States in 1939. He was a conductor and director of symphony and opera in St. Louis and many major Western cities. He became artistic director and conductor of the Western Opera Company in Seattle and, a year later, in 1964, he conducted the Seattle Opera Association's initial performance.

Weiskopf began his association with the POA by conducting "An Opera Gala" in Washington Park for three performances in the summer of 1966. The program consisted of music and song from seven operas. Under Weiskopf's direction, the POA presented Portland's first "Fidelio (Beethoven) and first "Flying Dutchman" (Wagner) in almost 70 years. He also scheduled, before his death in 1970, Verdi's "The Masked Ball," which had been absent 50 years.

Stefan Minde's association with the POA began with the 1970–71 season, in which he conducted the five operas selected by Weiskopf. Minde was born and educated in Germany. At the invitation of Boston Symphony conductor Erick Leinsdorf, he came to the United States in 1968 to study and work with Leinsdorf at the Berkshire Music Festival at Tanglewood, in Lenox, Massachusetts. Later the same year, he was engaged by the San Francisco Opera to conduct Mozart's "The Marriage of Figaro" and Donizetti's "L'Elisir d' Amore." Aside from his work with the POA, he had guest conducted the Oregon Symphony and is kept busy conducting operas in other cities in the United States and Canada.

A vast repertoire has enabled Minde, as it did Weiskopf, to present Portlanders with operas seldom, if ever, performed here. With the completion of the 1973–74 season, Stefan Minde has introduced Portland to its fourth operatic premiere in as many years—Strauss' "Ariadne auf Naxos," this past season's final production; Wagner's "Tristan und Isolde" in 1973; Strauss' "Der Rosenkavalier" in 1972, and Puccini's "La Rondine" in 1971. Next season, Minde has scheduled Strauss' "Salome," absent for 50 years, and Carl Maria von Weber's "Der Freischutz," performed here just once, more than 80 years ago.

Minde has come up with another "first," which may prove the Portland Opera Association's shining hour in the eyes and ears of opera lovers the world over. He has scheduled for the 1975–76 season the American premiere of Ernst Krenek's opera "The Life of Oreste," and the Austrian-American composer will be in Portland to celebrate both the premiere and his 75th birthday. This rather daring programming has paid off handsomely. The 1972–73 and 1973–74 seasons were sold out.

7.21.74

EUGENE'S VERY LITTLE THEATER

Dorothy Velasco

As legend has it, The Very Little Theater in Eugene was born and named on March 3, 1929, when eight enthusiasts met to form a community theater. One person declared, "There are hundreds of little theaters up and down the country, but this is certainly going to be a very little one."

This fall (1978) the Very Little Theater, otherwise known as VLT, begins its 50th anniversary season. According to anniversary activities director Scott Barkhurst, "We're not sure if VLT is the oldest community theater in the United States, but it is certainly one of the oldest. I'd like to make that claim and see if anyone challenges us."

The company is unique in that it has continuously functioned for 50 seasons, has always been self-supporting, and operates out of its very own theater building. It is doubtful that any other community theater in the country can duplicate all those claims.

The company's first production, Sir James Barrie's "You and I," opened on May 16, 1929, at the old Heilig Theater, a legitimate theater, which also served as a movie house. Gerda Brown, to this day an active member and occasional actress, was installed as VLT's first president.

The primary objective of the company was, and still is, to provide an after-work opportunity for local amateurs to strut their stuff before appreciative friends and regular theater-goers. However, several veterans of VLT, among them David Ogden Stiers of TV's "MASH," Edgar Buchanan of "Petticoat Junction" and Broadway actress ElMarie Wendel, were happy to use the company as a stepping stone to a professional career.

In 1931 VLT moved into the Pillbox, a small converted drugstore near the University of Oregon campus on 13th Avenue. For five years the struggling company managed to survive by producing either melodramas or classics, since royalties for newer plays were too expensive. It was during that time that VLT started its extraordinary collection of authentic late 19th and early 20th century costumes. "Since they were doing so many classics," Barkhurst explains, "members were instructed to go out and raid their grandparents' attics. Now our costume department is the envy of every other theater company in town."

After the confinement of the tiny Pillbox, VLT enjoyed 15 years of success in an old exhibition hall at the Lane County Fairgrounds. In 1950 the group was able to purchase a lot at 24th Avenue and Hilyard Street from the city of Eugene, and accepted bids for the construction of its present building, designed by a VLT member who was an architect. Much of the construction material was donated by various members.

"You could say that melodramas built the Very Little Theater," Barkhurst says. "Corn shows are always the most popular. There have been five different productions of 'The Drunkard' and five of 'Ten Nights in a Bar Room.' That doesn't mean that VLT does nothing but corn. Other recent productions include 'The Price,' 'The Andersonville Trial,' 'The Lark,' and 'A Doll's House.' Ever since the 1930s members have been debating over whether to produce comic melodrama or serious classics. We took an audience survey which showed an overwhelming preference for comedies, musicals and mysteries."

Usually a happy balance of corn and classics is achieved each season, keeping 600 or 700 subscribers as well as individual ticket buyers happy. Very few of the 200 seats in the theater ever go empty, in spite of competition from the University Theater, Lane Community College's razzle-dazzle musicals, Oregon Repertory Theater and the New Mime Circus.

Probably the best time in the history of the company was in the early 1950s, just before television became widespread. By the early 1970s VLT's directors took a good look at themselves and discovered that the mean age of company members was over 40. They decided it was time to bring in some new blood, and today there are 60 active members of all ages. Potential members must prove themselves by working on three different shows in three different categories, such as acting, set construction or publicity.

The Very Little Theater's 50th anniversary season begins appropriately enough with a corn show, "Aaron Slick from Pumpkin Crick," directed by Postmaster Ethan Newman of Eugene, who directed his first VLT production back in 1939. Four other plays will follow, as well as special anniversary events, including a banquet for all members, past and present.

VLT has maintained a pioneer spirit through all these years. "We have never wanted to accept money from grants or room tax funds, and I think that has a lot to do with our survival," Barkhurst says. "If we became dependent on outside help we might lose the spirit of self-sacrifice and the desire to pitch in and stand on our own two feet. No one is getting paid. We have no pretensions about being a professional group. We're just people of different ages and backgrounds who have a common bond, the enjoyment of doing a job as well as possible."

11.26.78

EXCERPTS FROM NOTEWORTHY STORIES

The Man Behind *The Fixer*
by Harold Hughes
10.9.66

"In his conversations with this writer, via telephone from Cambridge, Mass., [Bernard] Malamud exhibited the same warm, crisp style of talking that marks his writings. Asked if he saw any political similarities between Kiev and Corvallis, he quickly make it clear that he found no parallel, no reason to compare the narrow political thought of czarist Kiev with the free society of a small town in Oregon.

"But in *A New Life*, a novel critical of the lack of dedication to scholarship of the English department at Oregon State, the 'politics of the English department foretold a deeper involvement in *The Fixer*,' he said.

"'That man is by nature political, sometimes gets lost in the shuffle of daily living,' Malamud said.

"'But I wouldn't want anybody to get any idea that Corvallis or the faculty are not politically concerned,' he added.

"He said the lack of concern he saw at OSU during the late 1950s was for the humanities and has largely been changed for the better.

"...In *A New Life* there was considerable bed-swapping among faculty members. One English professor put a sign on his door after the book came out. It told the tittering students who read the novel, 'It wasn't my wife.'"

Film Censorship in the '50s—A Retrospective
by Chuck Boice
8.5.73

"It was 1952...For Portlanders, it was the last year they had 'full protection' against the dangers that lurk in motion pictures and stage shows. It was the last year of full operation of the Municipal Board of Review.

"The board's more than three dozen volunteer viewers— and one-man paid staff—checked every feature motion picture that came to Portland for possible public viewing. Sometimes this ran as high as 90 films a month. All had to be seen so the films could be cut or banned if they were 'deemed to be indecent, immoral, obscene, suggestive, immodest, untrue or designed or tending to foment religious, political, racial or social hatred or antagonism or which is deemed detrimental to the public peace, health, and welfare,' to quote the city ordinance of the time concerning motion picture and entertainment supervision."

The Dreams of a Genius
by Wilfred Brown
9.21.75
"[Eugene O'Neill] dreamed of using the Pacific Northwest as the backdrop for a new line of creation in the field that had made him one of the world's great literary masters.

"On that day in 1936 [the year he won the Nobel Prize in Literature], O'Neill talked with us not about his gloomy tragedies, but recalled with pleasure the acclaim given one very different play that recently had been made into a movie: 'Ah Wilderness,' a nostalgic, happy piece set in a New England town of a day he remembered from his childhood.

"And O'Neill talked of why he was then living in the Pacific Northwest, and of his plans for the future. He had projected in his mind a series of eight plays involving several generations of one family, carrying its people from New England across the Middle West and along the Oregon Trail to the Pacific Northwest. He looked forward, he said, to getting to work on the series.

"Those dreams of which he spoke apparently took written form in part, but they never reached the stage or print. Not many years later, O'Neill was stricken with a rare disease…

"Not long before his death at age 65 in 1953, [his wife] Carlotta reported, O'Neill insisted on destroying every fragment of his uncompleted and unpublished manuscripts…Whatever he had done on the Pacific Northwest series was included in the destruction."

Are the Arts Being Ignored by the Media?
by Hilmar Grondahl
7.4.76

"A few months ago, Martin Mayer, the distinguished music columnist of *Esquire Magazine*, wrote his last piece for that publication. Its editors didn't think their readers cared that much for his views on music and records. There is to be no replacement.

"And consider what happened at the Associated Press. For 15 years, Mary Campbell had covered the music beat for AP, and her wire stories had been used widely by member papers. Mary was recently transferred to business news and is now doubling as feature editor and women's editor.

"The head of AP's feature department has declared, 'All culture is (expletive deleted).' "

Bluegrass Is Booming In Oregon
by Charles Denight
7.24.77

"By Sunday morning the lawyers, accountants, musicians, et. al., who made up the bluegrass bands had begun showing beards. There was a relaxed joviality. The group on stage represented a mix of all the bands, and the feeling was fun. Between familiar gospel tunes the singers dropped country jokes and the crowd guffawed.

"The gospel crowd, the kids, the middle-class grown-ups all looked familiar. The scene resurrected memories of years in Southern Illinois, where on a Sunday morning the television dial flipped from a station in Kentucky, to a station in Southeastern Missouri, to one in Southern Illinois and they were all singing gospel tunes. The hair was shorter and the singers older, but the image was the same. Let's twang in the name of the Lord and have a little fun. Those were country people and so were some of these—and a lot more were trying to get back there, to that togetherness spirit. Perhaps that's where the popularity of this music form is to be found, in the cultural hoopla that accompanies bluegrass. The open smiles, the "Howdee" greetings, the unamplified music (you can talk with your neighbor during a bluegrass concert) must appeal to a segment of the young and not so young, reviving, perhaps, a friendlier American spirit."

The Theater Workshop: Its Time Has Come
by Charles Deemer
12.17.78

"[Mildred Hughes] and Portland composer Richard Moffatt founded the workshop as a response to the early years of television. 'The talent shows then kept using the same performers over and over. They didn't have anyone else. There was a real need for a training facility and an opportunity to perform on television.'

"...'We thought there wasn't anything we couldn't do,' Ms. Hughes told me. 'We did original musicals, plays and operas on KGW-TV. This was all done live in those days, of course. Sometimes we'd be called in at the last minute to fill in for a program that was cancelled. We had no lack of energy, and we also had the encouragement of Dorothea Lensch, who headed the park bureau. She gave us magnificent support.'

"...The 1950s were a golden age for Portland television for those who would demand of local productions something more ambitious than a talk-show format. For Mildred Hughes and the workshop, original theater on TV was all part of a very busy schedule."

seven:
The Lighter Side

"My Gubernator Platform"
by Rick Rubin
*"Well, the first thing I would do is install enormous
rolls of barbed wire all around the state."*

"The Creation of Oregon"
by Larry Leonard
*"Now of all the beasts of the field that Tom had
made, none was more subtle than the developer."*

MY GUBERNATOR PLATFORM

Rick Rubin

Now the campaign is well along, and try as I may I can no longer put off stating my aims. In fact, or course, my primary and perhaps only aim is to be elected Gubernator, but somewhere along about now I'm expected to tell you what I'll do if I'm elected.

The fact is, I have no idea what I'll do. How can a man know what he'll do until he has to do it? Yet it is the candidate's sacred duty to give the voters a few lyrical flights of campaign poetry, some dreams and fantasies to argue about with Pat the Barber or the little lady or the boys in the back shop.

Well, the first thing I would do is install enormous rolls of barbed wire all around the state. The goal of this daring scheme is to return the population of our little blackberry patch to about the 1940 level.

We'll station guards at each exit, armed with appropriate local weapons: Brush hooks, cross-cut saws, gill nets and umbrellas. These guards, of course, won't actually be able to keep anyone out. That would be unconstitutional, and I don't think we're ready to secede from the union quite yet. Can you imagine some nutty general marching from Prineville to the sea, trying to destroy everything in his path?

No, but the guards can stand there looking ferocious and when a tourist comes along they can try to get him to sign an oath promising not to settle in Oregon.

Meanwhile there'll be a steady stream of people going out, young kids who want to join the twentieth century out there in Disneyland, straight shooters who want to get on to the important business of life, like earning ulcers and piling up retirement funds, folks who don't like our climate and dream of a land where it's always 71.5 degrees and they can wear a Hawaiian shirt day and night, and those who don't like our rustic joys like hunting and fishing and being alone, who believe that the only good forest is a dead one. I'll instruct the guards to tip their hats as such folks pass out.

On the same general subject, I want to cut down on news of the outside world. I feel that the United States and nearly two hundred million people are too much to deal with all at once. They've been reporting every murder in the country for so long that I'm beginning to think everyone is a potential murderer, and though that may existentially be true, it's bad for my mental health.

Economy will be a big plank in my campaign platform. I think I can easily prove that I'm more economical than my opponents. Consider this: They have to pay for their publicity, and give away things like buttons and posters free. While I, on the other hand, am actually paid to write this stuff, and if I can't sell my posters there simply won't be any. How's that for economy?

One of my first economies when I'm elected will be finding high-paying jobs in government for my friends. That may sound like patronage to you, but it'll save the state considerable money, for my friends will then be off welfare and unemployment compensation.

Meanwhile I'll be fighting greedheads wherever they pop up. Greedhead loggers, greedhead fishermen, greedhead businessmen and all the other kinds of greedheads. I sometimes define greedheads as anyone who makes more money than I do but don't worry, the Gubernator gets $21,500 so your income won't be higher than mine any more and I won't bother you.

I want to see the state spring for a Gubernator's mansion, and I'm going to be quite nasty until something's done about it. I understand that Mark's wife had a go at that, but she gave up too easily. Who could withstand the governor of the state and his wife picketing the state legislature? Or chaining themselves to a pillar?

I'll repel outside industry, of course, and battle river pollution like crazy. I'll fight smog and the sales tax, swing for a stadium, and EXPAND THE STATE'S PRIMITIVE AREAS. In fact, I may see what I can do about making the whole state into a primitive area.

On a more general basis, let me assure you that I'll prayerfully consider every important decision, just like Mark. I promise to be responsive to the people, to take numerous polls to see what the voters want. I've already picked out my personal statistician, for though I'll take the polls I don't want them to interfere with my personal prejudices. A good statistician can prove that I'm following the popular mandate no matter what I do.

One of my strongest appeals will be to minority groups. I want equal opportunities for everyone. The first group I'll help will be the WASPs (WHITE ANGLO-SAXON PROTESTANTS), a minority group I've always wanted to see get equal treatment. In fact, if we can get them equal treatment I believe the rest of us minorities will be in such good shape we won't need any more help.

Behind all my promises I count on the rain. You can make a lot of mistakes in Oregon, at least in Western Oregon where most of the mistakes are made, but if you just walk off and leave the mistakes to fend for themselves, the blackberries and the Douglas fir will take over, and soon the people passing by will say: "Mistake? It looks like the rest of the jungle to me." There's always hope in Oregon as long as the nice wet rain falls on the nice fertile ground.

It has been suggested that a vote for me is a vote against the twentieth century. I agree heartily so much so that I plan to put the slogan on my campaign poster. For the twentieth century seems to me to be going in an almost uncanny number of wrong directions.

So much for promises. Now on to what really counts. Graft and corruption.

Graft and corruption? You thought we did away with all that, didn't you? Well, not quite. Politicians don't steal much any more, but that doesn't mean that they wouldn't like to.

They're human, just like you and me. Like us they are held back mostly by cowardice. Always pick a coward for your elected leader.

Still, I'm not going to be your Gubernator forever. Mr. Eisenhower has his farm, Mr. Johnson is a poor country school teacher no longer, and why shouldn't I feather my nest against the future? Surely you wouldn't want an ex-Gubernator on Aid to Dependent Children?

Luckily, I'm a poor man, my tastes are modest, and though I know you'll want me to have the best, the cost will not be high. And of course my attorneys will research carefully so that all the graft is strictly legal.

Since the state is too pinch-penny to provide one, I'll have to buy or rent a house first thing. Of course, since I'll have to live in it, I want the house to be a nice one. Once I've appointed my friends to high positions, they'll be dropping over to discuss state business, and we'll sit around talking and belting one or another beverage and watching TV, and I want the furniture to be nice. Also I'll want the best machines in the kitchen for Carolyn, and maybe I can figure a way for the state to spring for some power tools in the basement.

And any Eastern Oregon rancher who wants to invite me out to blast an innocent deer, or slaughter some ducks for the freezer, or any industrialist who wants me along out there on the salmon fishing trip, why just send that invite right along. I know, as do the voters, that you're not seeking any special favors, boys, you just like to chum with a good guy like the old Gub. Where seldom is heard a discouraging word, and the benefits flow in quite naturally.

So start memorizing the spelling of my name, because you'll want to write it in come November. R-I-C-K R-U-B-I-N. Be creative: Don't just mark an X, write in two whole words.

4.24.66

(Note: Mark Hatfield was Governor of Oregon from 1959-1967.)

THE CREATION OF OREGON

Larry Leonard

In the beginning Tom created the heaven and the earth. And the earth was without form and void (similar in some respects to Orange County, Calif.) and darkness was upon the face of the deep. And the spirit of Tom moved upon the face of the television.

And Tom said, "Let there be light," and there was a Bonneville Power Administration.

And Tom saw the light and did not turn Independent, and he divided the light from the darkness.

And Tom called the light Republican and the darkness he called Democrat. And the evening and the morning were the first day.

And Tom said, "Let there be a firmament in the midst of the waters, and let it divide the waters from the waters."

And Tom called the firmament heaven. And the evening and the morning were the second day.

And Tom said, "Let the waters under the heaven be gathered together under one place," and this place he called Oregon.

And Tom gathered the dry land together, and he called most of it California and some of it Arizona, although all of it falls quite nicely under the genre: dust.

And Tom said, "Let California bring forth grass," which it did to a staggering degree. Arizona, however, only brought forth cactus, which is painful to smoke. And the evening and the morning were the third day.

Well, this kind of thing went on for quite a while, what with fowl that may fly above the earth and great whales and cattle and creeping things (which Tom called conservatives) and such. But something was missing.

And so Tom said, "Let us make man in our image, after our likeness. And let him have dominion over the fish in the sea and over the fowl of the Democratic left and of the Republican right and over all the earth and every creeping thing, whatever its political affiliation."

So Tom created man in his own image, in the image of Tom created he him; male and female created he them.

And Tom blessed them, and said unto them, "Be fruitful and multiply," and they took him at his word and got right down to business.

And the evening and the morning were the sixth day, and it had been one hell of a week, so he createth "Mork and Mindy" and "The Rockford Files" and he tooketh a break.

Monday morning, first thing, Tom planted a garden in Oregon; and there he put the man whom he had formed.

And out of the ground made Tom to grow every tree that is pleasant to the sight and good for food and for clear cutting. The tree of life, also called the tree of knowledge of good and evil, he setteth on a nicely terraced spot with a view.

And a river went out of Oregon to water the garden, and from thence was it dammed until it did not move by the first man whose name was Col. Slackwater of the Army Corps of Engineers.

And Tom took the man and put him into the garden of Oregon to dress it and to keep it.

And Tom commanded the man, saying, "Of every tree of the garden mayest thou freely profit.

"But of the tree of knowledge of good and evil, thou shall not profit. For in the day that thou profitest thereof thou will be up to thy knickers in hot water."

And Tom said, "It is not good that Col. Slackwater should be alone; I will make a help mate for him."

Slackwater thought this to be a capital idea, and suggesteth something along the lines of a Julie Christie, but Tom caused a deep sleep to fall upon Slackwater, and he slept; and he took one of his ribs and closed up the flesh instead thereof.

And from the rib, which Tom had taken from Slackwater, made he a woman who resembled Ruth Buzzi. And Tom looked upon her and saw that it wasn't good. But he saith that every show on Broadway cannot be a hit. And so it was with this woman.

And they were both naked, Slackwater and his wife, and were not ashamed, but merely repelled. So Slackwater took up jogging and Buzzi got a Meier & Frank credit card and adorned herself with expensive raiment marked down from $39.95.

Now of all the beasts of the field that Tom had made, none was more subtle than the developer. And the developer said unto the woman, "Yea, hath not Tom said, ye shall profit of every tree of the garden?"

And Buzzi said unto the developer, "We may profit from all the trees of the garden.

"But of the fruit of the tree which is in the midst of the garden on the terrace with a view, Tom hath said, 'Ye shall not profit of it, neither shall ye sell it, lest ye scald thy knickers.' "

And the developer said unto the woman, "Ye shall not surely suffer loss.

"For Tom doth know that on the day thou sellest the property, thou shall realize a profit and be able to afford a condominium of thy own."

And when Buzzi saw that there was a buck to be made she had the papers drawn up and signed them. And she had Slackwater sign them, too, which he did willingly because the money would come in handy for a project he had in mind where he would buy up all the Laundromats and mix cement in them and dam the Pacific Ocean which at that time was moving.

And the eyes of them both were wide when they saw the cash.

And they heard the voice of Tom walking in the garden in the cool of the day. And Slackwater and his wife hid themselves from the presence of Tom amongst the survey stakes of the developer.

And Tom called unto Slackwater and said unto him, "Where art thou?"

And he said, "I heard thy voice in the proposed parking area, and I was afraid, because the title hast not yet cleared, and I hid myself."

And Tom said, "Who told thee that thou hast title to deliver? Hast thou taken a flyer and profited from the tree of life and knowledge that I satteth on the terrace with a view?"

And the man said, "The woman whom thou gavest to be with me, she setteth the deal in motion and covereth all angles including certain tax shelters and I did sign."

And Tom said unto Buzzi, "What is this that thou hast done?" And the woman said, "The developer beguiled me, and I did sell."

And Tom said unto the developer, "Because thou hast done this, thou art from this day a serpent cursed above all cattle and above every beast of the field, upon thy belly shalt thou go, and the dust of California shalt thou eat all the days of thy life, even unto the Sepulveda Interchange, dust shalt thou eat."

Unto the woman he said, "I will greatly multiply thy sorrow and give thee 50 detergents to choose from, and all shall claim to be best, and none shall remove the ring from around the collar."

And unto Slackwater he said, "Because thou hast harkened unto the voice of thy wife and profited of the tree of which I commanded thee, saying, 'Thou shalt not profit of it,' cursed is the freeway for thy sake.

"In sorrow shalt thou drive of it all the days of thy life, and cursed is thy lawn. Thorns also and thistles shall it bring forth to thee, and crabgrass.

"In the sweat of thy face shalt thou eat thy Big Mac and thy TV dinner, till thou return unto the ground."

Therefore Tom sent him forth from the garden of Oregon, to live in the San Fernando Valley.

So he drove out the man, and he placed at the south end of the garden of Oregon nine months of drizzle which turned away the most.

And for the rest, he removed the offramps from Interstate 5 so that all might drive right through to Washington.

Amen.

3.18.79

(Note: Tom McCall was Governor of Oregon from 1967 to 1975.)

AFTERWORD

In May, 1982, Joe Bianco left *Northwest* magazine to become Director of Special Projects for *The Oregonian*, where he remained until 1994. Retirement is not in Bianco's vocabulary, however. After his newspaper career, he became a book publisher, founding his own company, Bianco Publishing.

In 1984, the magazine's format changed to slick paper, giving *Northwest* a very different glossy look. Book reviews and fiction were added.

By 1991, *The Oregonian* was ready to call it quits, following the lead of other urban dailies in abandoning its Sunday supplement. Some of the magazine's content moved to a new full section of the paper, called "Northwest Living."

AWARDS

Some of the awards won by **Northwest** *magazine*:

1969: National Conference of Christians and Jews, Certificate of Recognition

1969: Thomas L. Stokes Award, Special Citation for series of articles on the environment

1970: Izaak-Walter League of America (Oregon Division), Golden Bear Award to Joe Bianco for environmental reporting

1971: Anti-Defamation League of B'nai B'rith, Human Rights Award

1975: University of Portland, Doctorate of Humane Letters to Joe Bianco

1980: Durham & Dunway, Inc., Best Seller in Northwest Award, *Mt. St. Helens — The Volcano* (Joe Bianco, editor); 250,000 copies sold

1981: George Foster Peabody Broadcasting Award to KATU-TV for television documentary on aftermath of Italian earthquake (Joe Bianco, co-producer, director, narrator)

ABOUT THE AUTHORS

Don Berry—Berry is best known for his novel *Trask*, which Northwest literary scholar Glen Love called "the best novel ever written and set in Oregon." Another novel, *Moontrap*, was nominated for the National Book Award. Berry spent his later years on Puget Sound's Vashon Island, where he gained a reputation as a creative genius, writing music, poetry, and children's literature and designing home computers. He passed away in 2001.

Joseph R. Bianco—Bianco began his newspaper career in Pennsylvania, where his crime reporting earned him a Pulitzer Prize nomination. After serving as agriculture editor at *The Oregonian*, he edited the resurrected Sunday supplement *Northwest* magazine from 1965 to 1982. Bianco finished his career at *The Oregonian* as Director of Special Projects, retiring from the paper in 1994 and starting his own publishing business. Among Bianco's honors and awards are a Doctor of Humane Letters from the University of Portland and a Peabody Award for co-producing, directing and narrating a television documentary.

Art Chenoweth—Art Chenoweth is a great grandson of Justin Chenoweth, who settled in The Dalles in 1849. Born in Portland in 1923, he began writing for newspapers in grade school. A graduate of Reed, he hired on as a sports writer and later news writer at *The Oregon Journal* in 1949. He was a regular contributor to *Northwest* for three decades and also has worked in television, radio, and advertising. Recently Chenoweth has worked as a news writer and columnist for Portland State University's *Vanguard* newspaper. In his 80s, he has no intention of retiring.

Larry Colton—Colton has contributed to *Esquire, Sports Illustrated* and *The New York Times Magazine*. He is the author of the acclaimed books *Goat Brothers* and *Counting Coup*, which in

2000 was nominated for a Pulitzer Prize. Colton is the founder of Community of Writers, a non-profit program to bring writers to Portland-area schools. As a young man, Colton briefly played baseball with the Philadelphia Phillies until an injury ended his career.

Charles Deemer—Deemer's books include *Selected Stories*; a novel *Love At Ground Zero*; a memoir, *Dress Rehearsals: The Education of a Marginal Writer*; *The Seagull Hyperdrama*; and *Seven Plays*, which was a finalist for the Oregon Book Award. Over four dozen of his plays have been produced, including *Christmas at the Juniper Tavern*, which won an ACE award for its public television version, and *Famililly*, winner of the 1997 "Crossing Borders" International New Play Competition.

Ivan Doig—Doig is perhaps best known for his memoir of family and landscape, *The House of Sky*, which was nominated for a National Book Award. His other books include *Dancing at the Rascal Fair*, *English Creek* and *The Sea Runners*. In 1989, the Western Literature Association honored Doig with its Distinguished Achievement Award for his body of work.

Charles Gould—Gould writes: "Charles Gould is a Portland writer." The editor adds, a busy and good one for decades.

Larry Leonard—Leonard is the editor of the online *Oregon Magazine*. He writes: "The first article I ever wrote was an early Sixties piece about striped bass fishing in the Millicoma River on Oregon's south coast. It ran in the Coos Bay World (a daily newspaper) with the headline 'Striper Fiver.' It was supposed to be 'Striper Fever,' but the ITU press room boys, all of them left-wing union thugs, intentionally screwed it up because they despised conservatives. Tom McCall was probably a member of AFTRA, but he wasn't a union thug. He was a big, lumpy liberal out of (where else?) Massachusetts—and according to his sister,

Dorothy, was the best 'wet hand milker' in the county when he was growing up. It is said that when he read the 'The Creation of Oregon,' he ran hooting and hollering through the KATU newsroom, holding the piece high above his head. He was the only liberal I ever knew who had a sense of humor."

Barry Lopez—Widely praised and honored author Lopez is the author of *Arctic Dreams*, which won the National Book Award. His other books include *Of Wolves and Men*, *Field Notes* and *Light Action in the Caribbean*. One editor has said about his work, "He nourishes us in a way we very much need, trying to restore our sense of place, our sense of humility in the face of the natural world. He wants us to regain our sense of direction and our sense of how to live well."

Ellis Lucia—Among the late Ellis Lucia's many books of Americana are *The Saga of Ben Holladay*, *Klondike Kate*, *Owyhee Trails* and *The Big Woods*.

Paul Pintarich—Pintarich is a third-generation Portlander, born in Portland in 1938; A graduate of Lincoln High School, Portland State College (as it was then); Navy veteran and former newspaperman, who worked nearly 30 years as a reporter and book review editor for the *The Oregonian*. In 1992 he was a recipient of an honorary award from the Oregon Institute of Literary Arts, and now is a free-lance writer, editor and poet.

Gerry Pratt—Pratt writes that he is "the only longtime reporter at *The Oregonian* to leave the place without a farewell cake-and-cookies party. Pratt always claimed it was because they hated to see him go. Others said it was because nobody noticed he had left. He was once fired by the late publisher Mike Frey because Frey didn't like what he wrote from Viet Nam. Dick Nokes, the city editor, and Bob Notson, the managing editor, rehired him."

Rick Rubin—Rubin has published over fifty short stories, many in such national magazines as *Esquire*, *Playboy* and *Argosy*, as well as hundreds of non-fiction works. He is the author of *Naked Against The Rain*, the definitive account of the first people of the lower Columbia River and of the Europeans who "floated ashore." Rubin was born and raised in Portland.

Dorothy Velasco—Springfield author Dorothy Velasco has written over thirty plays produced around the United States and in Canada, Mexico and London. Her outdoor drama, *Oregon Fever*, played for eleven summers at Oregon City. She co-authored the feature film *Raising Flagg*, starring Alan Arkin, and wrote and co-produced several award-winning video documentaries, including *The Roads Less Taken*. She has written for *Northwest* and many other magazines, and she is the author of several books about local history.

Ferris Weddle—The late Ferris Weddle is probably best known for his book *Tall Like a Pine* and his hundreds of outdoor articles, many published in *Northwest*.

Daniel Yost—Daniel Yost has been a screenwriter and director in Hollywood for 20 years and is best known for *Drugstore Cowboy*, which he co-wrote with Gus Van Sant. He recently returned to the Northwest to co-found a film company, Cascade Sky Entertainment.